ASPCA kids

bringing friends together,
paw in hand

Kids
Making a
Difference
for Animals

Nancy Furstinger

Dr. Sheryl L. Pipe

WILEY

Wiley Publishing, Inc.

Howell Book House
Published by Wiley Publishing, Inc., Hoboken, New Jersey

Photo credits: Inge Denehin: 2, 13. Jean Fogle: 4, 10, 22, 36, 50, 62. Lisa Medina: 6. ©iStockphoto.com/Emily Rivera: 7. ASPCA: 9, 11, 23, 33, 49. Clay Myers: 12. ©iStockphoto.com/Anna Utekina: 14. ©iStockphoto.com/Joan Vicent Cantó: 15. ©iStockphoto.com/Greg Nicholas: 16. Jill Carr: 18, 29. Nick Beaven: 20. ©iStockphoto.com/Connie Alexander: 21. ©iStockphoto.com/Chris Rose: 24. ©iStockphoto.com/Mark Hayes: 26. Augusta DeLisi: 27. Stacie Wogalter: 31. ©iStockphoto.com/suemack: 34. ©iStockphoto.com/Diane White Rosier: 35. Christine Distefano: 37. ©iStockphoto.com/Debi Bishop: 40. ©iStockphoto.com/Luis Santana: 45. ©iStockphoto.com/Günay Mutlu: 47. Ayna Agarwal: 51. Skye Bortoli: 53. Purestock: 54. ©iStockphoto.com/Phooey: 55. PhotoDisc/Getty Images: 57, 66, 67, 77, 83, 84. PhotoDisc, Inc.: 58, 74. Pier Pagano: 59. ©iStockphoto.com/Cheryl Bradley: 64. image100: 68. ©iStockphoto.com/Małgorzata Ostrowska: 69. ©iStockphoto.com/Tom Grundy: 70. Marty Snyderman/Corbis Digital Stock: 71. ©iStockphoto.com/David H. Lewis: 72. Monteverde Conservation League: 76. ©iStockphoto.com/Mark Kostich: 78. ©iStockphoto.com/Ryan Bolton: 80. ImageState: 82.

For general information on our other products and services or to obtain technical support please contact our Customer Care Department within the U.S. at (800) 762-2974, outside the U.S. at (317) 572-3993 or fax (317) 572-4002.

Wiley also publishes its books in a variety of electronic formats. Some content that appears in print may not be available in electronic books. For more information about Wiley products, please visit our web site at www.wiley.com.

Library of Congress Cataloging-in-Publication Data:
Furstinger, Nancy.
    ASPCA kids : kids making a difference for animals / Nancy Furstinger, Sheryl Pipe.
        p. cm.
    Includes index.
    ISBN-13: 978-0-470-41086-8
    ISBN-10: 0-470-41086-8
1. Animal welfare—United States—Juvenile literature.
2. Young volunteers in social service—Juvenile literature.
3. Social action—Juvenile literature. 4. Service learning—Juvenile literature. 5. American Society for the Prevention of Cruelty to Animals—Juvenile literature. I. Pipe, Sheryl. II. Title.
    HV4708.F87 2009
    179'.3—dc22
                                    2008046671

Printed in China

10 9 8 7 6 5 4 3 2 1

Book design by Erin Zeltner
Book production by Wiley Publishing, Inc. Composition Services

*For the inspiring Virginia "Ginny" Kroll:
rescuer of an amazing assortment of animals
and writer of wondrous tales.*

Contents

To the degree that we come to understand other organisms we will place greater value on them and on ourselves.

—E.O. Wilson

We cannot do great things on this earth. We can only do small things with great love.

—Mother Teresa

My enjoyment of animals began with Happy, my first dog. She was energetic, loving, fun, and always available for anything—from racing me around the yard to lying quietly by my side while I finished my homework.

But it was the bird feeder at my window that opened up the mystery of it all. From just a few feet away I could watch these alert, colorful creatures nourish themselves while keeping a wary eye on everything around them. I had so many questions about the birds: What did they do all day? Where did they go at night? What happened to them during storms? I thought there ought to be a daily newspaper to report on what had happened the night before in my yard. Who had survived? Who hadn't?

These questions inspired me to observe more and read more about birds. Then I began to learn about other animals—chimpanzees, snakes, and whales—by reading books written by famous authors who spent their lives studying them. Jane Goodall's writing on chimpanzees was the most fascinating to me. But everything I read led to more questions!

My early interest in animals continued to grow. After college, I became involved in creating programs that teach people to care about animals, and then became director of an animal shelter in New Jersey. Other positions followed, and eventually I became president of the ASPCA—which stands for the American Society for the Prevention of Cruelty to Animals—the first humane organization in the United States. My childhood curiosity led to a career helping animals, and that enriches my life beyond description.

This past year, the 400-member ASPCA team not only saved the lives of thousands of animals in this country, but also enforced the laws designed by our society to protect animals. The mission of the ASPCA from 1866 until the present day is "to provide effective means for the prevention of cruelty to animals." One way the ASPCA does this is through education—through written materials for young people. The books that I read when I was young fed my growing interest in animals. I hope this book will do the same for you.

Edwin J. Sayres
ASPCA President & CEO

Compassionate Kids

erhaps you're wondering, "I'm just one kid. How can I make a difference for animals?" Throughout history, the power of one ordinary person has sometimes changed the world in extraordinary ways. The inspiring kids in this chapter used compassion to help combat cruelty and assist homeless animals.

After you read their stories, think about ways you can help to make a difference for animals. The list of Things You Can Do Today at the end of this chapter will give you some ideas.

To the Rescue

Middle school students in Louisville, Kentucky, are showing two Pit Bulls that life can be cushy despite a "ruff" start. In February 2007, dogs were taken from an illegal dog-fighting ring at Bad Newz Kennels, owned by former NFL quarterback Michael Vick. The 22 Pit Bulls were renamed Vicktory dogs and are being cared for and retrained at Best Friends Animal Society in Kanab, Utah. Now, these battered dogs are learning the joys of playtime and hugs.

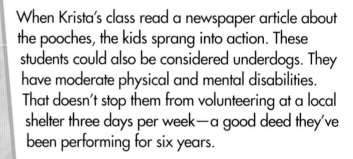

When Krista's class read a newspaper article about the pooches, the kids sprang into action. These students could also be considered underdogs. They have moderate physical and mental disabilities. That doesn't stop them from volunteering at a local shelter three days per week—a good deed they've been performing for six years.

The class decided to sponsor Little Red, a shy male Pit Bull. They also sent a care package to Georgia, a breeding dog who had all of her teeth pulled out. "We would love to send her a care package with toys and soft blankets and cards just to let her know how sorry we are for what she had to endure," Krista's class explains. "We want her to know that people all over this country care about her and want her to feel loved and safe."

Thanks to these special students, Little Red's and Georgia's hearts are healing along with their wounds.

Some Class Acts

The students at St. Catherine LaBoure School in Harrisburg, Pennsylvania, learned a lesson in kindness thanks to their involvement in Caring Classroom/Helping Hands, a community and service learning project for students in kindergarten through eighth grade. The eighth graders decided to adopt an animal rescue group as a pet project. They became animal angels for homeless dogs at Furry Friends Network, a group that rescues animals.

Students collected more than $1,100 in donations by holding a spare change drive and a pet photo contest. They collected wish list items such as pet toys and treats. And they helped host a very successful dog walkathon. Marissa says, "I learned how fun it is to volunteer. A lot of us in the eighth grade love animals. It's so nice to be able to help them."

Tony, another student, says, "We produce a closed-circuit television broadcast at our school. Sometimes the foster animals from Furry Friends come on our news program. One time I got to hold a puppy when I was doing the weather report. His name was Riley, and he was a Labrador Retriever mix. That's my best memory."

These dedicated eighth graders learned about pet care, pet overpopulation, volunteering, and fund-raising. Now they're teaching their schoolmates about caring for pets, bite prevention, and how to help homeless pets.

Students who attend the Theater Arts Production Company School in the Bronx, New York, are known for their creativity. Just before Christmas in 2006, the school's Tech Squad members used their imaginations to brainstorm a fund-raiser. Students decided to sell a variety of stuffed animals. The Tech Squad wanted to keep prices affordable: $4 or less. This would ensure that every student could buy a stuffed animal.

Sales of these plush creatures would help real animals. The students suggested donating proceeds to the ASPCA. "We chose to give to the ASPCA because we love animals," say Tech Squad students Amin, Marlon, and Alrinan. "They need homes and they need to be cared for, just like people."

Being theater students, the Tech Squad created a video explaining all about the ASPCA. Their video premiered at the school assembly. It was a megahit! And the fund-raiser was a smashing success. Students sold more than 350 stuffed animals. They donated $427 to the ASPCA. Bravo, Tech Squad!

A recycling project dreamed up by fifth graders at Fairfax Elementary School in San Bernardino, California, has created ripples. The students learned that the therapy dog visiting their classroom needed therapy herself. Kindra required expensive surgeries to repair torn ligaments.

The kids decided to start a recycling project. Bottles and Cans for Kindra helped make a dent in the dog's $6,000 vet bill. Then another school wanted in on the action. Third graders at Tokay Elementary School in Fontana, California, heard about the popular pooch and formed Friends of Kindra. They sold friendship bracelets to put another dent in the vet bill.

Others in the community have also pitched in to help pay Kindra's bill. And the incoming fifth-grade class at Fairfax Elementary School is continuing the legacy of Bottles and Cans for Kindra.

In Kansas City, Missouri, a fourth-grade class just had to take action. The students saw a photo in the local newspaper of a group of skinny Foxhounds with sad eyes. These neglected dogs had been seized from a man in Kansas City.

The kids started a campaign called Give Money for Food for Those Tail Waggin' Dudes. They publicized the Foxhounds with fliers and announcements over the school intercom. Kindergarteners broke open their piggy banks, and other students and neighborhood folks dug deep into their pockets. The class raised more than $900 to enable the local shelter to care for the Foxhounds. They deserve an A+ for awesome achievement!

Saving Strays

Sadly, homeless cats and other creatures roam neighborhoods searching for food and shelter. Four siblings rescued a feline family and offered these streetwise strays a second chance. Joanne, Malcolm, Jay Frye, and Nevaeh discovered the cats in their Philadelphia backyard. There were three tiny kittens huddled in a cinderblock while their mother hunted for food.

The siblings hatched a plan. If they could catch the cats and get them to a shelter, then the feline family could be put up for adoption. The kids didn't count on the kittens leading them on a wild goose chase!

One frisky feline zoomed out of the bush, hissed and scratched, then jumped off a ledge into a trash can full of rainwater. The kids raced to save the kitten from drowning. Soon he was snuggled in a sweater.

It took an hour, but the siblings caught the entire cat family. They reflected on why the rescue was such a big deal.

Nevaeh, 5, says, "I help save cats because I love them." Jay Frye, 12, and Malcolm, 13, both explained that they save animals because they don't want to see them struggling to survive on the streets.

Their big sister, Joanne, 24, who was in charge of the rescue operation, says, "I see so many people mistreat their animals, and I wish I had the authority to do something about it. I think that one person really can make a difference, and one day I hope that's me."

These kids have already made a difference. They adopted one of the kittens they rescued.

ASPCA Day

On April 10, animal lovers around the world dress in orange to celebrate the anniversary of the ASPCA. Even the Empire State Building in New York City is lit up in orange—the society's official color—to celebrate its founding way back in 1866.

In Añasco, Puerto Rico, an entire school went orange on ASPCA Day. Students of Parcelas Marias Elementary School learned about the ASPCA's mission to save animals. The young animal lovers read a story about a boy who adopted a homeless puppy. They discussed animal cruelty and agreed that people need to be responsible by protecting animals around the world.

Then students showed their true colors. The kids tied orange yarn around their wrists. They created anticruelty signs and dipped their hands in paint to decorate the signs with oodles of orange handprints.

In Red Bank, New Jersey, Shaylyn went all out on ASPCA Day. The teen showed her spirit by wearing an ASPCA T-shirt and wristbands. She decked out her dogs in orange bandanas and enlisted her brother's help. They paraded around the neighborhood wishing everyone a happy ASPCA Day.

The day before, Shaylyn had hand-delivered letters and wristbands to neighbors so they could celebrate the special day too. She also held an ASPCA fund-raiser at her school, passing out more wristbands to those who donated. "Most girls my age are more concerned about clothes or boys," Shaylyn says. "I am concerned about the animals."

Justine, 10, celebrated the 142nd birthday of the ASPCA in 2008 by giving gift bags of goodies and information about animal welfare to her class. She then delivered an informative talk about the ASPCA.

That evening, Justine held a fund-raiser and collected $285. People also signed pledges against animal cruelty. The star of the night was a stuffed dog named Bruno, displayed alongside a poster outlining different types of animal abuse. Justine empowered her fellow animal lovers by including information about organizations to contact to help fight animal cruelty in their neighborhood.

The Business of Helping Animals

Molly might be young, but that hasn't stopped her from starting a business to help animals. The Pittman, New Jersey, 6-year-old started Molly Knox Pet Socks. Her rhyming venture recycles old socks into catnip toys.

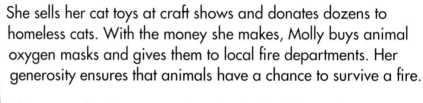

She sells her cat toys at craft shows and donates dozens to homeless cats. With the money she makes, Molly buys animal oxygen masks and gives them to local fire departments. Her generosity ensures that animals have a chance to survive a fire.

This young businessperson has inspired adults to donate oxygen masks—ranging from kitten-sized to big enough to fit a Bull Mastiff—to fire departments in other towns. This small girl has had a big impact!

After Sharlynne heard about a therapy pooch who needed surgery, she channeled her creative talents into helping this distressed dog. Sharlynne has always had a big heart and a generous spirit. When the 12-year-old visited a local humane society in California, she saw a badly injured dog. She donated a box of pennies to help pay for medical expenses and promised to raise more money.

Later, Sharlynne learned that Havoc, a Rottweiler who is both a therapy dog and a reading assistance dog, needed costly surgery. The dog had a tumor and her surgery would cost more than her family could afford.

This spurred Sharlynne to start Crosses 4 Critters. She designed and created beaded crosses and other jewelry, raising $200. But she didn't stop there. Sharlynne inspired her community to raise more than $14,000 for Havoc's surgery. Recently, Havoc celebrated her 10th birthday and is back at work.

Crosses 4 Critters continues raising money to help creatures in need of veterinary care. Sandy, the cat of a 92-year-old woman, got the surgery she needed, thanks to Sharlynne's efforts.

Jillian celebrated her Bat Mitzvah in a delicious way when she turned 12 years old. She decided to raise money for EmanciPET, a nonprofit spay/neuter clinic in her hometown of Austin, Texas. Jillian began baking and selling yummy treats for people and their pooches.

Orders poured in, and the young baker didn't stop until she made 70 bags of cookies and 54 bags of dog treats! "I had to be diligent in order to raise the funds to achieve our goal," Jillian says. "One of my sponsors, Nora Lieberman, helped out by eating all the rejected cookies."

Perhaps Jillian's pooch, Feebee, ate the rejected dog treats. A photo of Jillian and Feebee graced the label on her treats. She raised nearly $5,000 to help combat the pet overpopulation problem in Texas.

"Jillian is a great example of how anyone can make a difference for animals, and how young philanthropists are changing the world," says Amy Mills, executive director of EmanciPET. "Her story shows that it's not your age or the size of your bank account that matters—it's your creativity and passion for helping animals."

When Disaster Strikes

When Hurricane Katrina struck New Orleans in 2005, it turned into a double disaster. The wind and rain did terrible damage. Then the local lake flooded and residents had to leave their homes. Many were forced to leave their pets behind.

Many kids worried about the thousands of lost and injured pets roaming New Orleans after the hurricane. Isabelle wanted to help the homeless animals, but what could an 8-year-old in Washington State do?

Plenty, it turned out. Isabelle got a local store to donate boxes of dog biscuits. Then she partnered with Cingo, her Labrador Retriever–Blue Heeler mix, to sell the treats. Together they raised $200 for the ASPCA Disaster Relief Fund. Four paws up for this team!

Math, science, and drafting were put to the test when students in the Design and Challenge program in Charlottesville, Virginia, decided to help dogs who lost their homes after Hurricane Katrina. Fifth through eighth graders took a professional

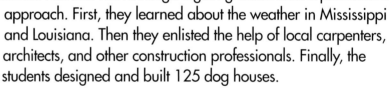

approach. First, they learned about the weather in Mississippi and Louisiana. Then they enlisted the help of local carpenters, architects, and other construction professionals. Finally, the students designed and built 125 dog houses.

The kids coined a new word—*barkitecture*—to describe their unique creations. One resembles a bright red fire truck complete with wheels and ladder. The Princess Dog House is a castle fit for a female canine. The Sphinx is pyramid shaped. There's even the Thomas Jefferson Monticello, updated with solar-powered lights and heat sensors for a pooch with political aspirations!

All of the dog dwellings were donated to animal rescue groups on the Gulf Coast. The students say, "We're very proud of our work and we would like to keep helping dogs in the future."

Animals with Special Needs

Many rabbits are dumped in the weeks following Easter because, unlike a chocolate bunny, real rabbits require special care. Shoji, 19, discovered an abandoned domestic rabbit in his Torrance, California, backyard. When he caught the brown bunny, Shoji discovered that his rear legs were paralyzed.

Shoji decided to adopt this bunny with special needs and named him Roger. The teen lovingly cares for Roger, exercising his hind legs and giving him what rabbit caregivers call "butt baths." He even goes home between classes to change Roger's bunny diaper! Roger's veterinarian praised Shoji's dedication, saying he is more dedicated than some parents.

Shoji explains why he is so devoted to Roger. "If you decide to accept living things into your home or family, you should take care and never ever abandon them for being who they are. Take responsibility. If you are thinking of getting a rabbit or any animal, adopt them from a local animal shelter."

RabbitMatch, a shelter that rescues and finds new homes for house rabbits, featured Roger's story in its newsletter. Two women from Heartland Rabbit Rescue in Oklahoma read it and called Shoji. Their disabled bunny, Murphy, had died recently, and the women wanted to donate his wheels to Roger.

The women had bought a tiny cart designed to help paralyzed dogs walk. Shoji's dad helped adjust the miniature cart, guaranteeing that Roger will be able to zip around faster than a jackrabbit. This big-spirited bunny won the rabbit lottery when he hopped into Shoji's heart!

Did you know that cats with white fur and blue eyes may be born deaf? When Erika adopted 3-year-old Snowflake from the Rescue House in San Diego, she knew her new pet faced a special challenge. Deaf cats can be scared, confused, or grouchy. However, they learn to rely on their super senses of smell and touch (especially with their whiskers) to get around.

Twelve-year-old Erika relied on vibrations to communicate with her new cat. "Snowflake doesn't hear, but she feels vibrations. When I enter the room, I slam the door very hard. She feels the vibration, turns around, and sees me coming. Stomping my feet also works," she says. "If Snowflake is sleeping on my bed, I slowly enter the room and gently rock the bed. She then wakes up and sees me."

Erika is also teaching Snowflake hand signals. "She's learned that if I hit my leg, she should come." It will be interesting to see what else Snowflake can learn.

Penning a Protest

When was the last time you were passionate about preparing for an exam? When Fiona Paterna prepared her seventh-grade classes for writing persuasive essays, she switched on the television. Students in West Deptford Middle School in New Jersey watched *The Oprah Winfrey Show*. The April 2008 episode investigated the secret world of puppy mills—commercial farms where puppies are bred in large numbers for sale in pet stores.

The shocking conditions the mother dogs endure as they give birth to more and more puppies for pet store profits upset Paterna's students. "It's just not right," says Summer. "They don't get fed enough or walked on grass, and they're skinny as anything."

Thomas agrees. "It was sad how they treated these dogs. I was like, 'Wow, how could they do that?' It should change."

All 36 students tried to change things using the power of the pen. They wrote letters to state officials demanding that changes be made to the state law to make it tougher on puppy mills.

The seventh graders didn't stop there. They made T-shirts with the slogan "Stop Puppy Mills." Then they put on the shirts and filmed their own segment for Oprah Winfrey, mailing the tape along with a T-shirt. Give those students an A+ for a great group effort!

Learning More

Twice a year, a new generation of animal advocates can spend a week at the ASPCA Mini-Camp for Kids. Kids ages 7 and up gather at the Staten Island Children's Museum. There they discover how to harness kid power to benefit animals in New York. Campers learn about the role of animals in our lives, being prepared for disasters, shelter animals, pet training, and more.

Special guests at a recent camp included the Smile Retrievers—four Golden Retriever therapy dogs who helped comfort victims of the World Trade Center terrorist attack. Dogs Jake, Jesse, Mattie, and Macie demonstrated how wagging tails have the power to heal broken hearts.

In fact, Victoria and Christina spread a lot of cheer with their smiling Goldens. Instead of hitting the mall on weekends, the sisters visit sick children and grieving families with the Smile Retrievers.

The Delta Society, an organization that tests and certifies therapy animals and their human partners, certified both girls as junior dog handlers. This allows them to participate in pet partner programs with their four dogs. Victoria, 11, and Christina, 13, say that seeing their Goldens bring smiles to sad faces "is a wonderful thing."

Victoria and Christina say they plan to continue community service with their dogs "forever." They hope that their enthusiasm about volunteering inspires more of their friends and schoolmates to also get involved. Now that's a lesson those campers won't forget!

Things You Can Do Today to Make a Difference

- Brainstorm a fund-raiser with your class. How about a Dog Day Afternoon in a local park with fun activities such as a pet and person look-alike contest, a doggy relay race, or a paw-paint art gallery? Sell tickets and donate the profits to a humane society. Don't forget to advertise well in advance by hanging posters and contacting the media.

- If there's an animal shelter or sanctuary near your school, ask school officials if your class can tour it during a field trip. Set up a donation box a week in advance to collect food and toys.

- Celebrate ASPCA Day throughout the year by reading books about animals to younger students. Go to www.aspca.org/bibliography for a list of hundreds of books about animals that the ASPCA recommends. Pick stories that emphasize treating animals with respect and kindness.

- Partner with your well-behaved pet to visit patients in hospitals and nursing homes. Join a visiting pet group to get involved. (People and animals who participate in pet therapy need to be tested and registered through the Delta Society, www.deltasociety.org, Therapy Dogs International, www.tdi-dog.org, or another group.)

- Invite a humane educator or other animal welfare official, such as an animal control officer, to give a presentation at your school. Find out how you can help prevent and report cruelty to animals. (See www.aspca.org/cruelty to learn how to report animal cruelty in your area.)

- Speak up for animals. Make posters encouraging people to adopt a homeless pet from the shelter. Design a bulletin board featuring photos and brief bios of adoptable pets (remember to update it weekly). Set up an information table with ideas (such as these!) about things your classmates can do to make a difference for animals in your community. Write letters to your school newspaper about animal issues.

2 Shelter Helpers

Kids are making a big difference for animal shelters across America. Banding together or working solo, children of all ages raise funds, volunteer, and foster animals in need. They have opened their hearts and donated their time and money to homeless animals.

Volunteering Precious Time

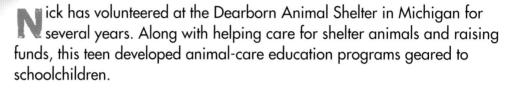

Nick has volunteered at the Dearborn Animal Shelter in Michigan for several years. Along with helping care for shelter animals and raising funds, this teen developed animal-care education programs geared to schoolchildren.

"I believe that volunteer work is the most important thing that anyone can do, no matter what organization or mission you volunteer for," says Nick. "My passion is for animals and speaking up for them because we are their voice. I became a volunteer at the Dearborn Animal Shelter because I wanted to give back to my community."

And give back he did, logging a record number of volunteer hours—more than 2,000. In fact, the shelter decided to lower the age requirement for employment. In 2007, Nick became the shelter's office assistant.

Nick also manages to squeeze in time as the director of the Friends' Teens for Animals Project. Its focus is to educate teens and get them involved in making a difference for animals in their communities. If anyone can encourage these young people, it's Nick!

At the Mollywood Parrot Rescue and Sanctuary in Bellingham, Washington, parrots who were once pets are guaranteed a lifetime of love. All of the parrots were abused, neglected, or turned in by people who were unable to give these intelligent birds the special care they require.

The flock of more than 400 feathered friends considers Heidi their champion. This 17-year-old started volunteering at the sanctuary in 2001. She's become skilled at feeding and medicating the birds.

"I'm not proud of what the human race has done to take them from their natural habitat," Heidi says. At Mollywood, the parrot's wild nature is respected.

Heidi helps spread the word that captive parrots make challenging pets. She gives presentations to middle school students. Part of the fun is showing kids how to make hanging bird toys.

Alexa has loved dogs nearly all of her life. When Alexa turned 10, she was looking at an adoption web site and saw that some dogs were scheduled to be killed when homes could not be found for them. "I immediately started crying to my mom that I wanted to save dogs," the East Haven, Connecticut, teen says.

"I started fostering dogs on my 11th birthday. The first was a Labrador Retriever who came off a bus that came up from a southern state. She was covered in her own waste and was skinny and scared, but I could tell in her eyes she already trusted me."

Since that day, Alexa has fostered other dogs for Labs4rescue, a nonprofit organization specializing in rescued and homeless Labrador Retrievers and Lab mixes. In addition, she raises funds for shelters and rescue groups, and volunteers at a Rottweiler rescue called Cathy's Rottie Rescue Rehab and Sanctuary.

Alexa adores senior dogs. "One day my dad brought me to pick up our newest foster, who was a senior," she recalls. "He ranted about how 'old dogs don't do anything but die, and this is your last senior foster.' However, he ended up adopting that same dog, who has been with us for two wonderful years."

Her current foster dog has cancer, but has been fighting the disease and has already lived longer than anyone expected. Her bravery has inspired Alexa to someday become a veterinarian.

Creative Fund-Raising

A fifth-grade class at Crystal Springs Elementary School in Bothell, Washington, wanted to raise money for homeless animals during their fall dance. So they came up with a sweet surprise.

Students invented a tasty slogan: Eat a Sweet, Save a Life. Then they baked some delicious desserts and sold them at the dance. They raised $120—enough to microchip 24 cats and dogs at the PAWS shelter. A veterinarian can inject a tiny microchip about the size of a grain of rice under a pet's skin between the shoulder blades. The number on the microchip is registered in a database with the pet parent's contact information. If the pet ever becomes lost, veterinary clinics and humane societies can use special scanners to read the microchip's number, match it with the pet's information, and then reunite the pet with her family. Now that guarantees a happy ending!

A class of first graders at Harvest Elementary School in Fresno, California, proved you're never too young to help homeless animals. They raised $649 for Valley Animal Center as part of the shelter's fund-raising campaign to collect spare change. These students dug deep to contribute more pocket change to the campaign than anyone else.

Students at Lincoln Park Elementary School in New Jersey also turned their pocket change into money for their local shelter. They celebrated Kindness for Animals Month by dropping coins into collection bins. The money multiplied! At the end of the month, the kids' generosity resulted in a check for $605.49 being presented to Montville Pet Parents, a volunteer organization dedicated to building a kinder world for pets. The school's Parent Teacher Organization matched the money. The donation will go toward building a new animal shelter in Montville. A celebration wall will feature a plaque saluting this special school.

A student at Seattle's Salmon Bay Middle School came up with an innovative idea to help animals. Catherine created Sun Puppies—a group that hosts fund-raising dog walks. The young girl wanted to support rural animal shelters. Participants put their best foot forward on the first walk, raising $750. Part of the donations paid for a critically ill puppy's surgery.

The student council of Stewart Elementary School in Stevensville, Michigan, came up with a unique way to raise money for the local Benton Harbor Humane Society. They invented Slipper Day, where students could wear slippers to school. But everyone who wanted to wear slippers to school had to pay $1. Thanks to great team spirit, the students raised $199 plus donations of cat litter, food, and dog treats.

Fourth-grade students at Lincoln Elementary School in St. Joseph, Michigan, hosted a We Love Animals Drive along with a Valentine's Day candy sale. What sweet success! The kids collected more than 700 items and $100 for the Humane Society of Southwestern Michigan.

A special songbird is singing her heart out for the animals. Nikki, 12, performs classic songs by famous vocalists such as Nat King Cole to raise money for homeless pets. Audiences applaud Nikki and her generosity. When the girl sings out, both the ASPCA and the Friends of County Animal Shelters in Bergen County, New Jersey, benefit.

"I feel bad when I see puppies without homes and I wanted to sing to help them," says Nikki. Now that deserves a standing ovation.

23

Making Things for Animals

Girl Scout Troop 1477 from Eanes, Valley View, and Cedar Creek elementary schools in Texas brought their sewing baskets to Town Lake Animal Center in Austin. These self-proclaimed "pet-crazy girls" made hand-stitched cat beds and toys. The Girl Scouts also took shifts in the shelter's cat house during their Monday sewing parties, to spend time with the cats.

As a bonus, the girls got to watch the shelter cats batting the toys and snuggling in the beds they had made. Many of the cats got adopted and took along their beds to have sweet dreams in their new homes.

The crafty girls earned their bronze award—the highest recognition a Junior Girl Scout can achieve. Isn't that the cat's meow?

Animal lovers Nick, Will, Joelle, and Quinn dreamed up a purr-fect project for community service. They made fleecy hammocks for Heart of the Catskills Humane Society in Delhi, New York.

The kids agreed it was heartwarming to see kittens cradled in the hammocks. As a bonus, these hammocks won a blue ribbon at the Delaware County Fair in New York State.

Finding Forever Homes

Girl Scouts in Troop 1441 from Phoenix, Arizona, get lots of sloppy kisses from the animals they help. The 11- and 12-year-old girls have pledged to find homes for dogs and cats in their local shelter.

At monthly adoption fairs, the scouts work in shifts. They ask potential adoptive families questions, walk the dogs, play with the cats, keep water bowls filled, and clean up. The girls have also collected 32 enormous sacks of dog and cat food, along with donated toys, chews, crates, and blankets.

Jordyn, a fairy godmother for felines, has found homes for more than 100 cats. The cats are from Last Hope, an all-volunteer animal rescue organization that is dedicated to saving abandoned and unwanted animals. Last Hope offers cats and dogs a safe sanctuary through a network of foster families until they find forever homes.

Jordyn started fostering cats and kittens for the Farmington, Minnesota, pet rescue group when she was 15. "In the summer of 2004, I discovered four kittens living under the shed in my backyard. We initially contacted Last Hope in hopes that a volunteer would arrive at our doorstep, catch the kittens, and take them into a home to foster them for us," Jordyn recalls.

But it was kitten season—the time when stray cats everywhere give birth. "All of the volunteers had more animals in need of homes than they could handle," Jordyn says. A volunteer from Last Hope told Jordyn's family how to safely trap the kittens, who were then brought to the veterinarian for vaccinations. The teen and her sister persuaded their parents to foster the litter of four kittens. They soon were joined by five others kittens along with the mama cat.

"After many weeks of socializing, nurturing, and attending Adoption Days, we successfully placed all 10 cats in loving homes," Jordyn says. Since the kittens were feral (born wild), they had very little human contact and needed to be socialized so they would learn to trust people and become good pets. (Socializing means slowly introducing the kittens to new things and new people in a way that doesn't cause them stress.) "Soon after, my family realized how fun and rewarding fostering homeless animals could be." Jordyn's family can now proudly state that they have found forever homes for more than 100 homeless, abandoned, and abused cats and kittens.

When she's not busy filling up her foster home with adoptable cats, Jordyn uses her artistic talents to help Last Hope. She's designed a snazzy new logo and Adoption Day signs to help get more animals adopted.

Jordyn also created educational pamphlets and wrote articles addressing a variety of animal topics. This innovative teen has tackled "the importance of spaying and neutering, the joys of becoming a foster parent for homeless animals, how adopting homeless animals makes a positive impact on pet overpopulation, and the unpleasant issue of puppy and kitten mills."

When 9-year-old Wyatt visited a Wauchula, Florida, animal shelter to donate food, he met Sasha, a black Labrador Retriever. He learned that the shelter no longer had room for Sasha, and she was scheduled to be killed.

Wyatt refused to let that happen. However, his family already had four dogs. Determined, Wyatt scraped together birthday, tooth fairy, and report card money to pay the adoption fee and returned for Sasha. She became his first foster dog. Then he marched into the local newspaper office and asked the publisher to feature Sasha.

The boy built a kennel for his foster pooch and invented a cool name for his group: Wyatt's Ruff Rescues. Sasha didn't stay long—she was adopted in a week.

Wyatt returned for a German Shepherd Dog. Each time a dog was adopted, Wyatt would return to the shelter and pull out another death-row pooch.

Rescuing dogs is "ruff" work, especially since Wyatt does it all. He feeds and trains his dogs and even names them by calling out a selection of possible names to see what they answer to. He holds yard sales to raise funds and gets donations from adopters.

This resourceful boy has adopted out nearly 200 dogs (plus 20 cats). "There's always one that I hate to give up for adoption," Wyatt admits. "But I just think about how they're going to a better place than the shelter, and it makes me feel better. That's what matters." His huge heart is helping him make a humongous difference for some very lucky dogs.

Augusta read an announcement on PetFinder, a national pet adoption web site, that eight dogs in West Virginia had only five days to find homes before they, too, would be killed for lack of space in their shelter. The 12-year-old jumped into action—even though she lived in Pittsburgh.

"I discovered that I had to do something about it," Augusta says. "I knew that I could not just sit back and let this happen. I knew that if I could just get those dogs to my house, I could find them homes."

On that September day in 2002, the girl and her family drove to the shelter and brought home the eight dogs, who were a mixture of breeds and ages. At the end of the five-hour round trip, Augusta found safe spots for the dogs and kept on going.

She named her nonprofit pet rescue Augies Doggies Rescue and filled it with foster dogs. Most arrive from crowded shelters in rural Ohio and West Virginia. Augusta selects the dogs based on who needs the most help. She asks how much time the dog has waited in the shelter to be adopted and when the death date is scheduled.

Fund-raisers such as Pennies for Pound Puppies and Party for Pound Puppies help her pay for shelter adoption fees, vaccinations, spays and neuters, plus dog food, beds, toys, and treats.

What keeps her motivated after rescuing, fostering, and rehoming 110 dogs? "When I find they've been adopted, it's the best feeling ever," Augusta says. "There is no greater feeling in the world than to know you saved a life."

Although people tell her that she can't save all the animals, the teen always responds that she can try. "I believe that anyone can make a difference. Nothing comes easy, but if you give it your all, you can accomplish great things," says Augusta. "I was 12 years old the day of my first rescue, and yet that day seemed to define everything I am. I was not much more than a child, but I knew I wanted to make a difference, and that still remains today."

Augies Doggies Rescue has relocated near Chicago, where Augusta is a student at DePaul University. Along with school, she's busy building a new network and caring for her three dogs: Daisy, a Pembroke Welsh Corgi; Clover, a Pit Bull mix she rescued from West Virginia; and Roxi, a German Shepherd-Collie mix.

Big Business

Siblings Allison, 8; Lorelei, 6; and Ryan, 3 told their mother they wanted to raise funds to "help the animals at Best Friends," a sanctuary at Angel Canyon in Utah that is home to about 2,000 animals from around the country.

The sisters and brother set up a lemonade stand. They squeezed fresh fruit from their grandmother's lemon tree. They also sold fresh-baked brownies. The siblings raised $36.50.

Ian wears a suit and tie when he meets with his staff of more than 30. This big boss is only 8 years old, yet his business has raised more than $16,500 in three years.

Ian's Bead Company began as a sidewalk stand selling key chains made from pipe cleaners and colorful plastic pony beads. He earned about $12, and donated it to New Leash on Life, a Chicago dog rescue.

Sales snowballed and soon boys and girls started creating jewelry and gift items at craft parties. Now they host shows at an upscale store. Ian's staff includes a CEO (Chief Earring Officer) and a CBO (Chief Barrette Officer).

The young entrepreneur has appeared on a variety of talk shows, including *The Martha Stewart Show*. Ian won the American Humane's 2008 Be Kind to Animals Kid Contest, and gave away most of his prize money to three animal shelters.

Despite the fame, Ian's focus remains on his furry friends. He aims to "help dogs who don't have a home so they can get a better home. Kids can make a difference, not just adults," he says. "Kids can help animals and people so they can have a better life."

After watching a commercial showing caged shelter animals, Cady knew she had to do something straightaway. The 10-year-old from Westport, Massachusetts, loves horseback riding. One day she started sculpting small horse heads and attaching pins to the back.

Soon Cady was making an array of animal pins: dogs, cats, birds, pigs, donkeys, giraffes, elephants, and zebras. The gifted artist even used her Old English Sheepdog, Hobie, as a model. She sells the custom clay pins for $5 apiece under her label: Barnyard Benefits.

Cady chose the name to reflect her love of all creatures. "We have to protect all animals that no one takes care of," she says. "They are not to blame for their situation. They are innocent and need our help."

Cady has donated $1,000 to horse rescue organizations and local animal shelters. "People mistreat animals and that's not fair to them," she says. "Any way I could help them—it's the right thing to do."

Hands-on with Animals

Each day, Hannah, age 5, helps her mother, Stacie, at Lucky Paws Rabbit Rescue, an upstate New York bunny barn that is home to a rotating roster of about 30 rabbits. The young girl sweeps the hay-filled stalls and pours food into dishes. However, her most important job is to talk to the rabbits and play with them.

Most of the rescued rabbits are afraid of people because they have never been handled. They need gentle attention so they can learn to trust people and be adopted into new, loving homes.

One special rabbit name Starlight hopped into Hannah's heart. Now Starlight shares Hannah's bedroom and gets nightly bedtime stories whispered into her big ears. "I love Starlight," Hannah says. "She licks my hand when I pet her. She's a good bunny."

Fantastic Food Drives

When sixth graders Kayla, Terrian, Briar, Courtney, and Kayla learned that a local shelter needed dog and cat food, they got busy. The girls organized a pet food drive and fund-raiser at Ostrander Elementary School in Wallkill, New York. Their enthusiasm netted a huge haul: 456 cans and bags of pet food plus $433. That's a lot of kibble!

John Muir Middle School's 4-F (Fur, Fins, Fangs, and Feathers) Club decided to play Santa for homeless pets. The 35 club members hosted a December pet food drive and collected enough cans of cat food and boxes of dog biscuits to fill their sacks. Thanks to 4-F, holidays have been brighter for cats and dogs at Friends of the Fairmont Animal Shelter in San Leandro, California.

When the kids aren't collecting, they're meeting twice a month to learn responsible pet parenting from local animal professionals. Sounds like a great club to join.

When Mimi came across a web site that donates 20 grains of rice to help end hunger in Africa every time you visit, she wondered if the same thing would work for hungry dogs. "There are tens of thousands of dogs in animal shelters across the country, all needing to be fed a good meal," she points out.

The 12-year-old girl from Bend, Oregon, launched www.freekibble.com on April 1, 2008. Despite the date, the site isn't an April Fools' joke. It features a different dog trivia question each day. When a person clicks on the answer, whether right or wrong, 10 pieces of kibble are donated to a rotating roster of shelters.

The site is off to an incredible start. In the first month, Mimi raised enough kibble to feed 456 dogs at the Humane Society of Central Oregon for one day. That's a lot of chow hounds! "It was very fun and we can't wait till the next delivery," she says.

Mimi hopes that along with learning fun facts about dogs by playing Bow Wow Trivia, kids around the world will be inspired to spread the word about how homeless animals need help. The site now includes a page to feed cats, too.

Educating Others

Kristen started volunteering at the Hawaiian Humane Society in the heart of Honolulu for a Girl Scout project. When she learned that the society is devoted to promoting the bond between animals and humans, something clicked.

The teen decided to reach out to Hawaii's youngest population. She spent a year developing interactive lesson plans for preschoolers. The lessons were developed with the assistance of the society's education department and preschool teachers, and are designed to teach children humane values.

"I've always been interested in animal rights and caring for animals, and I wanted to teach younger children more about them," Kristen explains. She used her original sketches to create activity pages that

preschoolers can color. The budding artists learn why it's important to treat animals with compassion.

"Everyone deserves to be respected and treated fairly, and that way we can eliminate homeless dogs and abused dogs, as well as abused children," the teen says. That's an important lesson for all of us.

Students at Waukesha North High School hope to broadcast the benefits of spay/neuter surgery to curb pet overpopulation in their Wisconsin neighborhood. The teens, who are part of the Lead to Succeed program, gave presentations to community leaders about animal issues.

When students learned that cats were being killed because there wasn't enough space in shelters for all the kittens being born, they wanted to get the word out. "If we start at the beginning and limit the breeding, we can change the equation in hopes to balance it," the students stated in their presentation.

Their Don't Let the Cat Out of the Bag campaign stressed the importance of community involvement in the homeless cat situation. Students are spreading the word about how the local Humane Animal Welfare Society hosts an outdoor cat plan that spays and neuters barn and feral cats free of charge.

As the students emphasize, "Without humane education, there is little hope in changing the future."

Tehila asked guests to nix the gifts for her Bat Mitzvah and instead make donations to the Animal Rights Community of Greater Cincinnati. The group used Tehila's contribution to create the book *Care of Companion Animals* and distribute it free of charge.

A Special Place for Horses

Twelve-year-old Rachel cofounded the Amaryllis Farm Equine Rescue with her mother in 2005. Since then, this dynamic duo has saved 73 horses, ponies, and mules from a sad fate.

The animals they rescue are former family pets, race horses who no longer win, horses who worked hard all their lives but were never given the retirement they had earned, or wild mustangs roaming on public land where ranchers want to graze their cattle. All were headed to slaughterhouses. Their meat would be shipped to Europe and Asia for people to eat.

"I want to speak for the animals who cannot speak for themselves," says Rachel, a sixth grader at Stella Maris Regional Catholic School. Along with championing the cause, she also works hard to take care of the animals at the Southampton, New York, horse rescue group.

Before and after school and all summer long, Rachel can be found feeding, brushing, and caring for the horses and the many barnyard animals who have found their way to the safe haven. She makes sure all the animals get the pampering they deserve.

That includes horses like Pirate, a stunning young stallion who was rescued in the nick of time. The truck to the slaughterhouse arrived at the same time that the check did from Amaryllis Farm Equine Rescue to free Pirate. A group of mares— Pirate's mother and aunts—weren't as lucky. They boarded the truck.

Pirate and many other horses at the sanctuary are searching for loving, permanent homes on ranches and farms. More than 25 horses have been offered full sanctuary at Amaryllis due to age or special medical needs, and these horses need sponsors. In the meantime, Rachel lets all of the horses, ponies, and mules (along with the rescued pigs, ducks, and chickens) know how much she adores them.

To help Amaryllis Farm Equine Rescue save more horses, three generous girls refused birthday presents for the second year in a row. Instead, Olivia M., Madelaine, and Olivia B. asked for donations to be made to the farm. The trio donated $1,306 to help care for Captain Barbossa, a blind Appaloosa gelding. This horse is described as "a perfect gentleman who loves women." And three girls certainly love him back.

Things You Can Do Today to Make a Difference

- Sign up for your local shelter's volunteer program. You may walk dogs, groom cats, or play with rabbits.

- Become an animal angel by donating wish-list items. All shelters need canned food, leashes, toys, cat litter, towels, and cleaning supplies. Find a local shelter by searching online at www.aspca.org/findashelter or through Petfinder.com (go to "Animal Shelters by Distance" and type in your zip code). Or look in the Yellow Pages.

- Volunteer with rescued horses at a farm sanctuary. You may clean stalls, scrub water buckets, groom horses, or stuff envelopes with an appeal for donations.

- Instead of asking for more stuff for your birthday or holidays, why not start a new trend? Ask your friends and relatives to bring presents for homeless pets (dog beds, cat scratching posts, rabbit willow balls) and then distribute them to shelters.

- See if your school can hold a fund-raiser such as a bake sale (include dog biscuits). You could also ask if money made recycling cans and bottles can go to the local animal shelter.

- Start an animal club. Your club can create crafts for critters, such as catnip toys and pet placemats.

- Host a silent auction for animals. Ask friends, family, neighbors, and local businesses to donate handmade crafts and other items, gift certificates to restaurants and movies, and services such as pet sitting and dog grooming. Display photographs of the items and services, along with descriptions, on a community bulletin board and hang envelopes so people can place their bids. Remember to create a display of the animal charity where funds will be donated so bidders will dig deep into their wallets!

- Host a giant flea (no, not that kind) market. You can charge admission, or charge a fee for people to have tables in the market. Make it a smashing success by advertising for donated items to benefit shelter animals. Motivate people to clean out their closets, attics, and basements.

- Encourage everyone to prevent the overpopulation problem by spaying or neutering their cats, dogs, and rabbits. This simple, safe surgery eliminates health problems and unwanted litters. You'll save lives and your pet will be healthier and happier. Check to see if your local humane society offers a low-cost program, or call SPAY/USA at (800) 248-SPAY to find a nearby clinic that offers low-cost surgery.

- Adopt your next furry friend from an animal shelter or a rescue group. An incredible assortment of potential pets are searching for forever homes. Never shop at pet shops, which get animals from puppy and kitten mills. These commercial breeder farms churn out millions of puppies and kittens, while at the same time nearly 4 million animals are killed in shelters each year. Remember to shop only at pet supply stores that do not sell cats or dogs. And give your adopted pet a daily dose of love—the best gift of all!

- If your family can't make the commitment to care for an adopted animal for all her life, consider fostering. You can make all the difference for a homeless animal by providing a temporary home. The animal you foster will learn household manners, thus making it easier to find a forever home.

3 Animal Advocates

Some people think kids are too young to really make things happen. But many kids have a positive attitude and a belief in themselves, and they have used those qualities to change the world around them. They have turned innovative ideas into positive action for animals.

Starting an Animal Shelter

The seeds for a splendid idea started with newspaper photographs of dogs in shelters. Diane Trull, a fourth-grade reading teacher at Allyn Finch Intermediate School in Dalhart, Texas, used the local paper to encourage reading. On that day in March 2003, one of her students wondered what happened to the dogs if they weren't adopted.

Diane explained that the dogs would be killed because there simply weren't enough homes. Their city shelter in their tiny Texas town was killing 600 dogs a year.

Her fourth-grade class refused to accept this "solution" to the dog overpopulation problem. "Why do the dogs have to die?" students asked. "Can't we do something about it?"

Jesse asked, "Why would it be right to kill the dogs if the only thing they want is someone to love and they don't have a home? We don't do that to homeless people, do we?" These questions spurred Diane and her class to change the fate of more than 3,500 dogs plus 500 cats.

The idea for the Dalhart Animal Wellness Group and Sanctuary (DAWGS) was launched in their classroom. However, the school did not want to endorse the program. Diane said she and her students were not "derailed. We went to the city council to propose a plan to take dogs from animal control. They were very skeptical, thinking children could not make a difference and, if they did proceed, it would be a short-term venture. They agreed to give us the dogs and puppies after three days at the shelter."

Diane continues, "Two days later, the animal control agent showed up at the school with twelve dogs. He said we could either take them or they would be euthanized. We asked him to give us until the end of the school day and we would find a place for them. Several of the students convinced their parents to let them keep them for a few days and we were off and running."

DAWGS started off in a deserted building with a side yard that a local judge donated. Diane used her credit card and an account at the local hardware store to buy what she needed to start building pens at the new sanctuary. Within a month, the new residents settled into their safe haven.

From the start, this shelter broadcast the students' belief: "All dogs are equal, and each one has a special gift to give." They decided that no animal would be killed in their shelter just because he didn't have a home. Alix explains, "Dogs don't deserve to die if there's nothing wrong with them."

Scores of kids worked hard to make a difference for each of the dogs. Boys and girls raised money by recycling newspapers. Articles about DAWGS in *Best Friends* and *People* magazine spurred many small donations that have kept the shelter operating.

DAWGS had just welcomed its first residents when it had to relocate due to a zoning law. Diane and her students got busy once again, building kennels on a small plot of city land that included several outbuildings used back in the 1930s as a slaughterhouse. Every day after school, homework, and chores, and on weekends and holidays, these dedicated students arrived at DAWGS. They made sure that the dogs received food and water, clean bedding, exercise and playtime, and loads of love.

An assortment of homeless dogs—playful puppies and seniors with gray muzzles, purebreds and mutts—are available for adoption. All are spayed and neutered, resulting in a significant drop in the number of strays.

Diane pointed out that in 2003, DAWGS was "getting in more than 100 dogs and puppies a month. Today we average about 20, unless a large group of Labs come in. Their litters can be 12 or more! So I think the spay/neuter clinics are making a difference."

Alix adds, "I can't understand why people won't just take care of their animals. It would be so simple if they spayed and neutered. Then there won't be so very many that need homes."

The lucky animals who have been adopted from DAWGS share their happy "tails" through newsletters and on the shelter's web site. Angela, a terrier mix, became a movie star. She played the part of Daisy in the movie *Dr. Doolittle 3*. Buddy, a Golden Retriever mix who was one of the first shelter dogs, saved an elderly woman. But she returned him to the shelter when she installed a new pond in her garden that she didn't want him to swim in. A couple read about this hero pooch and decided to adopt him. Soon a private plane arrived to take him to his forever home.

The unconditional love of these dogs inspires students to volunteer. Kali explains that she volunteered with the dogs because "Well, I just love dogs. Everyone should!"

"I come here most every day," says Jesse. The boy invented a title for himself: TLC Coordinator. "I just love the dogs, and this is way more fun than other stuff."

His younger sister, Alyssa, said after an adoption of one of her favorites, "It makes me happy for the dog to finally find a great home, but it makes me so sad to see him go. These are tears of happiness. I love him so much, I know this is the best thing for him."

Many of the original fourth graders continued their involvement with DAWGS. New recruits help ensure that the safe haven continues.

Unfortunately, the shelter faced a new problem in December 2005 when city officials decided to close it down. DAWGS had six months to leave. The city said the noise of 500 dogs barking and howling was disrupting funerals in the nearby cemetery.

Fund-raising to save DAWGS kicked into high gear. Soon a new location was found, and work began on a new building. The city extended the move date. However, Mother Nature refused to cooperate. On moving day in April 2007, thunderstorms, rain, sleet, hail, snow, a blizzard, and even a tornado bombarded the region. But with kids, volunteers, and total strangers pitching in, more than 500 dogs and puppies snuggled into their new sanctuary.

Hannah, 8, observes that DAWGS resembles the little engine that could. "We just keep thinking we can, and finally we made it!" Now everyone knows that the DAWGS kids definitely can make a difference. They've beaten the odds—twice!

Lifesaving Vests for Police Dogs

cross North America, kids are helping protect police dogs by donating bulletproof vests to keep these canine heroes safe. In 1999, Stephanie read a newspaper article about K-9 Officer Solo, who was killed in the line of duty. The dog was a member of the Monmouth County, New Jersey, sheriff's department and had been following orders when a suspect shot him.

The story of the slain police dog haunted Stephanie, who was 11 at the time. "I was really sad," she remembers. "I don't think an animal should be shot. They're kind to protect us, so we should protect them too."

When she learned that the Associated Humane Society of New Jersey had raised money to get bulletproof vests for police dogs in the state, Stephanie decided to do the same. The Oceanside, California, girl made fliers explaining why she wanted to raise money to purchase bulletproof and stab-resistant dog vests. Then she decorated donation boxes that she placed at neighborhood veterinarian offices and pet supply stores.

Stephanie phoned the local newspaper to tell the reporter about her idea, which she called Vest-A-Dog. Her goal was to buy a vest for Tiko, a police dog in her hometown. Thanks to her hard work, she purchased Tiko's vest—and five more!

Stephanie was unstoppable. She continued her mission to get vests for all the dogs in San Diego County—more than 50. "I'm very surprised it has gone this far," she says. "In the beginning I didn't even think we'd get enough money for one vest."

Now Vest-A-Dog has gone nationwide. Stephanie's goal is to donate vests to every law enforcement dog in North America. She has bought a vest for thousands of dogs who faithfully protect people every day.

In Florida, a 10-year-old girl read an article about brave police dogs who put their lives on the line yet often go unprotected because of the high cost of police vests. Stacey marched into her local police department in 2000 and asked if she could collect money for the vests, which cost from $500 to $700 apiece.

Stacey's pet project became a nonprofit charity—Pennies to Protect Police Dogs. To collect all those pennies and other spare change, she made collection jars that featured a photograph of her and a police dog.

Then Stacey crisscrossed Florida to collect funds, and to deliver vests. She has raised more than $160,000 and purchased nearly 200 bulletproof vests. Despite recognition for her achievement, Stacey says, "I don't do this for the awards. I do it so that the police dogs get vested."

Kelly, another 11-year-old, founded the nonprofit organization Maine Vest-a-Dog in 2000. This dog lover was unable to have a dog of her own due to her mother's allergies. So she became involved in community service as a way to connect with canines.

Kelly's goal of providing bulletproof vests to all Maine police dogs was on its way to becoming a reality. The West Bath girl raised $50,000 and bought vests for 56 dogs. "Police dogs don't choose their lives, so they deserve to be protected," Kelly says. "The thought of police dog deaths was a lot to bear, and still is, when it could be prevented with a bulletproof vest."

Suddenly, an obstacle threatened to stop her mission. Kelly discovered that Maine law prohibited anyone from asking for funds to benefit law enforcement. Determined to change the law, Kelly worked with her state senator and testified before the Criminal Justice Committee. A new law passed in 2002 allowing nonprofit groups such as Kelly's to raise money for police departments.

Changing the Law

Like Kelly with her police dog vests, other kids have worked to change local laws in ways that benefit animals. Fifth and sixth graders in the Radcliffe Elementary School's Animal Club persuaded the mayor of Nutley, New Jersey, to officially approve a Care of Animals ordinance. Now dogs have basic rights. They must be given healthy food, clean water, and warm shelter. They cannot be tied out on chains shorter than 15 feet, nor can they be outside for longer than eight hours. People who break this law can be hit with a $5,000 fine and 90 days in jail.

Smart Chicago students proposed a No Canine Profiling resolution that targets irresponsible people, not pets. Four students at Brentano Math and Science Academy in Chicago won a contest sponsored by Illinois State Representative Toni Berrios. Eighth graders Natalia, Lysette, Yaritza, and Jasmine researched, developed, and proposed this new resolution.

The teens' canine-friendly legislation urged the state not to ban specific breeds of dogs. It encourages cities to pass laws targeting irresponsible pet caretakers and to establish programs that educate residents. These girls know that dogs, like people, are individuals. They should be judged on their deeds rather than their breed.

In Spalding County, Georgia, Naomi's mother was trying to get the county commissioners to encourage spaying and neutering by changing the county's animal control laws to require higher pet license fees for unaltered dogs and cats. Naomi, 10, went with her mom, Kelly, to a Spalding County Board of Commissioners meeting. During the public comment section of the meeting, each person was allotted up to five minutes to speak. Her mother was slotted to speak on one subject, and she had arranged for another speaker to read a speech she had written addressing another point. When the other speaker failed to show up on time, Naomi insisted on reading her mother's speech about how spaying and neutering doesn't destroy hunting dogs' ability to work.

Naomi was the hit of the evening. She cited several experts who are in favor of spaying and neutering hunting dogs for performance and health reasons. She got the most attention reading a statement from Dr. Vern Brock of Manito Veterinary Clinic. "I've never found a connection between a dog's nose and his testicles."

Then she handed out a stack of articles on the subject. She also emphasized that there is no need to breed hunting dogs. "Approximately *half* of all the dogs picked up by Spalding County Animal Control are hunting breeds or mixes of hunting breeds. And approximately 25 percent of all the dogs in the shelter are purebred dogs," Naomi informed her audience. In other words, if you need a hunting dog, go to the shelter and adopt one.

The young speaker says, "I was *really* nervous because I'm a little shy, and to have five stern-faced commissioners staring at me was a little unnerving. But I did what I did because the animals can't speak up for themselves, and it seemed like the right thing to do."

Along with giving spur-of-the-moment speeches, Naomi and her brother, Ethan, 7, helped their parents run a boarding facility for rescued animals. The family pulled dogs and cats from the local shelter, took them to a clinic for spaying and neutering (of course!), and cared for them until they were moved to other locations where they could find homes. The brother-and-sister team, who are home-schooled, spent hours each day taking care of their boarders. They played with the dogs and cats, even making toys for them, and cleaned litter boxes and dog pens.

"Sometimes it was a lot of fun," Ethan says. "We had one dog we boarded whose name was Corona. She was very playful and loved running and playing fetch. It was sad when Corona went away, but I'm glad we could help. I feel bad for all the animals who don't have homes, and I'm glad we help make a difference."

Taking a Stand

When Nessarose brainstormed ideas for the National History Day theme for 2006—Taking a Stand in History—her pets inspired her. The Kennedy Longfellow School student shares her home with three rescued cats and an Australian Shepherd.

"I have been interested in animal shelters and rescues ever since I adopted two cats," Nessarose says. It only seemed natural that her research project would focus on animals.

The Cambridge, Massachusetts, teen selected an inspiring topic: "Henry Bergh: Taking a Stand for Animal Rights." Bergh founded the ASPCA in 1866 to "provide effective means for the prevention of cruelty to animals throughout the United States."

In her presentation, Nessarose said Bergh's beliefs continue to be vital. "Teaching people not to abuse animals is so important," she stressed.

Clubs with a Mission

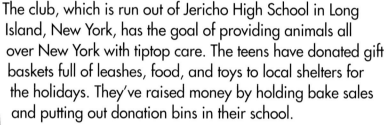

William wasn't discouraged when he discovered that he was too young to volunteer at the animal shelters in his area. "I took matters into my own hands," he says. The high school senior started Kids Helping Pets in 2003 to gather together teens passionate about animal welfare.

The club, which is run out of Jericho High School in Long Island, New York, has the goal of providing animals all over New York with tiptop care. The teens have donated gift baskets full of leashes, food, and toys to local shelters for the holidays. They've raised money by holding bake sales and putting out donation bins in their school.

After Hurricane Katrina hit, Kids Helping Pets donated $1,000 to Little Shelter Animal Rescue & Adoption Center. This New York shelter took in animals who had lost their homes because of the hurricane and were left stranded and starving in New Orleans.

Kids Helping Pets also encourages the next generation of animal advocates. The group took third graders to a local shelter so they could hang up a mural they had painted at one of their fund-raising events. "Since the younger generation is the future of animal well-being, one objective of our club is to teach the younger community about animal welfare," William says. That's an idea we all want to pass on.

In Tulsa, Oklahoma, the Tulsa County Paw Stars 4-H Dog Club has hooked up with Meals-on-Wheels, a program that delivers hot meals to needy people. Many senior citizens consider home-delivered meals a lifeline. They depend on daily Meals-on-Wheels deliveries and often share their hot food with their pets.

Now the Paw Stars 4-H Dog Club is making sure that these animal companions have their own healthy food. Kimberlie, a club member, wanted to work with pets for her community service. She approached Meals-on-Wheels, and Meals 4 Paw Starz was the result. Young volunteers deliver donated pet food to elderly and disabled people once a month.

These furry friends help connect homebound folks to the outside world. "I hope we can spread this throughout Tulsa," says Kimberlie. Hopefully this appealing idea will catch on across the country!

Kids are also reaching out to animals around the world. While visiting her family in New Delhi, India, Ayna, 16, noticed many homeless dogs. They were starving, disease-ridden, and missing paws. She was determined to take action.

"I clearly remember the sight of a puppy on the street rolling around in the middle of the road. He was hurt and everyone was going about with their daily lives. I was absolutely heartbroken," Ayna remembers. "No one wants to see dogs on the streets, looking and just waiting for a home and to be a good companion."

This heartbreaking situation spurred Ayna to start Stop Pet Overpopulation Together Globally. Her group focuses on raising money, and then working with community veterinarians to spay and neuter stray animals. A major part of the work she does is to educate the public about homeless pets. She instructs the workers and volunteers in developing Third World nations on proper animal care. Ayna is currently making a video to spread awareness to her community back home, along with the many other educational campaigns she runs.

"I absolutely love animals and would do anything to make them safe and happy," she says. "If there were enough people willing to care for all the animals, we wouldn't have to euthanize all these hopeful babies. So I thought that we should just control the population and I really wanted to work at a global level. There are so many ways that you can help animals, and I feel that this is one of the biggest needs in the world."

Back home, this Edison, New Jersey, teen volunteers at a veterinarian's office and at her local animal shelter, for which she also holds fund-raisers. In addition, Ayna is working on her Girl Scout Gold Award by opening a dog park in her community.

And if all of these animal activities aren't enough, she also ran a summer camp called Paws and Claws "to educate kids in grades three through five about animal welfare and protection," Ayna explains. "Kids can learn how to share the world with our furry friends." The camp was a hit, and it is officially being added as an annual program. Ayna will be running as well as directing this program. She hopes to spread this camp program nationwide as a part of the YMCA summer camps. "Personally, I think education is the best way to spread the message," she says.

Of course, Ayna has big plans for the future. "I hope to grow up to be a small animal veterinarian while raising money to travel for a few months across the world providing assistance to animals of all kinds," she says. Her dream is to open an animal shelter. Her goal is to "speak for the animals because they can't speak for themselves."

Defending the Ocean's Animals

Teens around the world have spoken up to save the beautiful creatures of the sea. An Australian schoolgirl flew to Alaska in 2007 and to Chile in 2008 to speak out at the International Whaling Commission meetings. Skye, the founder of Teens Against Whaling, is passionate about bringing an end to commercial whaling worldwide.

After volunteering at a whale festival when she was 11, Skye went on her first whale-watching trip. "It was the most amazing experience of my entire life, and since that moment I have never wanted to do anything else with my life." That experience motivated her to collect 131,965 signatures on a petition to end whaling, and then fly to Japan to present it to officials.

This dedicated conservationist keeps teens updated on her progress through her web site. She also funds her mission by hosting fashion parades, auction nights, family fun days, and car washes. Skye says, "The youth of the world are the ones who are going to be in charge of this fragile world one day, and unless we start working together, we are going to be handed an Earth that is broken beyond repair."

Meanwhile, a Florida teen has become a champion of loggerhead sea turtles. Zander is on a mission to prevent endangered loggerhead sea turtles from becoming extinct. When Zander was 11, he discovered that the number of turtle nests was lower than normal. The boy began volunteering to monitor turtle nests along the beach near his Florida home.

When he spoke to marine biologists, Zander learned that sea turtles are in great danger. "All the sea turtles are endangered or threatened," he says. "Their main predator is man." Pollution and beach trash harm their nesting areas, and fishing lines and nets injure the turtles.

The teen wanted to focus attention on the turtles' plight. Zander applied to the Gulf Coast Community Foundation of Venice and received a grant. With it, he launched his environmental education program for students: Turtle Talks.

Zander created a turtle costume to grab kids' attention. It combines a Hula-Hoop with a canvas shell that is attached to a backpack. Kids put the costume on as Zander gives a lesson on loggerhead anatomy. Then his young audience buries Ping-Pong balls in a sandbox to explore how turtles lay their eggs. His Turtle Talks inspire thousands of kids to help protect these prehistoric reptiles.

The turtle spokesman has taken his conservation program around the world. He created the *"Turtle Talks" Activity Book* to spread the message about protecting these ancient animals.

In Columbus, Ohio, Jennifer is dedicated to protecting sea creatures. The eighth grader learned that the six sea turtle species found in U.S. waters or nesting on U.S. beaches are designated as either threatened or endangered under the Endangered Species Act. So she sharpened her pencil and wrote world leaders asking them to protect turtles. Jennifer also gave presentations and raised $300 at a recipe contest held at Jones Middle School. She donated the money to the Earth Island Institute, a California organization that encourages people who are finding solutions to protect our planet. "My advice to any middle school student who undertakes a similar project is to persevere—and enjoy the reward of your effort," Jennifer says.

Some Mexican schoolchildren are also turtle lovers. They helped give 1,500 baby Golfina turtles a boost when they released the hatchlings into the sea. Each year starting in May, mother turtles arrive at the beach to nest. Each turtle scoops out a two-foot-deep hole in the sand, deposits about 100 eggs into her nest, covers the eggs, and then returns to the sea. Police and volunteers guarded first the eggs and later the hatchlings.

Golfina turtles are in danger of becoming extinct because people slaughter them for their meat, leather, and shells, and also steal their eggs. After 45 days of protection, the baby turtles took their first steps toward the sea, shepherded by the children.

Animals on the Internet

Lindsey's first visit to an animal shelter was a real eye-opener. "I couldn't believe there were almost 40 dogs and cats waiting to be adopted," says the 13-year-old from North Branford, Connecticut.

Lindsey already had an impressive volunteer record, helping out at a veterinarian's office and writing a weekly pet column for her local paper. But she felt it wasn't enough. "I wanted to do something more that would get *lots* of animals adopted," she says.

How could she help all those homeless animals find forever homes? "The shelters were so limited that I knew people couldn't get there," she says. Lindsey decided to bring the animals to the people. She snapped photos and wrote bios of cute, cuddly Connecticut cats and dogs. Then Lindsey got her mouse in motion, setting up a web site called Pet's Pal. "The web page enables people to look at the animals at any time," she explains.

Even though Lindsey has gone to shelters each week for two years to profile the adoptable animals, she admits it was difficult to get adults to believe in her. "I think now I'm finally being taken seriously," she says.

Thanks to this pal of pets, the future looks brighter for more than 200 animals who were adopted from 17 shelters because of Lindsey's web page.

Saying No to Dissection

Dissecting animals (killing a live animal and then studying its anatomy) was once required in science classes. Students who refused because they felt this practice is cruel were sometimes given a lower or failing grade.

The controversy over dissection in the classroom ignited in 1987 when a high school sophomore refused to dissect a frog. Jennifer, then 15, complained that frogs were being needlessly killed. The California teen protested on moral grounds.

Her objection intensified when her school refused to allow an alternative to dissection. Jennifer's science grade was lowered to a C. When she challenged her school's decision, the state court ruled that Jennifer should be given a frog that had died of natural causes to dissect. Jennifer appealed, suing her school. This courageous young trailblazer prompted California to become the first state to pass legislation protecting a student's right *not* to perform dissection.

The student choice law stirred other students into action. Maggie, then 15, refused for religious and moral reasons to dissect animals. Her New Jersey school gave her grades of zero for the biology assignments she refused to perform. Maggie sued the school in 1989 and won a settlement that required the school to provide her with alternative ways to do her science class work.

Many years later, another New Jersey teenager spoke out against dissection. Laura refused to dissect a cat in her freshman anatomy class in Washington Township High School. She testified before the State Assembly Education Committee. She didn't think it was fair that dissection was required in her state. Students who opposed dissection received a failing grade.

Laura's decision to speak up for the bill proved successful. The Student Choice Law passed in 2006, making New Jersey the ninth state to allow students the right to refuse dissection. "It is amazing to be involved in government that is for the people and by the people," Laura says. "It is a great feeling to be involved in the political process."

In Nevada, a sixth grader opted out of dissecting an earthworm. Laurie, a straight-A student, received a C in her science class. Two years later, and with more Cs for refusing to dissect animals, she took a stand.

Laurie asked students to sign a petition requesting an option to dissection. She took it to the Clark County, Nevada, school board. The student choice amendment, providing students with alternative assignments, passed in 2002.

"You don't learn anything about an animal by cutting it up," Laurie explains. "It's a waste when there are so many other ways to learn about science without having to kill something first."

Elijah also opposes dissection. Together with a friend, the high schooler started the New York student group Last Chance for Animals GHS (Guilderland High School) to champion animal issues.

"Our high school needed a group to bring concerned students together to fight for animals. I thought a high school group would be a great way to make a huge impact on the lives of countless individuals," says Elijah, who is now in his senior year.

The Guilderland High School group actively campaigned against dissection. "We had an intense anti-dissection campaign and have increased the number of students opting out. We've done video screenings, information tables, petitions, and letter writing," Elijah explains. He adds that Last Chance for Animals GHS also met with school officials and later teamed up with lawyers from Physicians Committee for Responsible Medicine "to threaten legal action when the high school refused to allow dissection choice for certain classes."

Their demonstrations and activism resulted in victory for both the animals and ethical students across New York State. The school district now recognizes a student's right to opt out of dissection and not be punished for making the choice.

Speaking Up

Rose, 7, champions an assortment of animal causes. In winter, whenever she spots someone wearing a fur coat or hat or something with fur trim, she'll ask her mother if it's real or fake. If it's not a fabulous fake, Rose will ask the wearer, "Were animals killed to make that coat?" Then she reminds the wearer that the only one who looks glamorous in a fur coat is the animal who was born wearing it.

The New York City girl also adores her rescue dog, Daisy. She tells everyone that Daisy is her sister! Rose asks people walking dogs whether their pet is a rescue. She understands that every dog who is purchased from a pet store represents a lost opportunity to save one from a shelter. If she finds out that the dog wasn't adopted from a shelter, Rose says, "There's a lot of dogs at the shelter that need homes, and they get put down if they're not adopted."

This miniature activist also protested when her class hatched baby chicks. She's working to get this misguided lesson stopped. Students can humanely learn about the life cycle of chickens by reading books and watching films. They don't have to hatch chicks, who become stressed without a full-time mother and usually do not survive in the classroom. The lucky chicks from Rose's classroom were sent to Farm Sanctuary in Watkins Glen, New York, where they are now free to scratch for worms.

Michael leaped into action when he learned that his high school was planning a Kiss the Pig contest during the annual Powder Puff football game. The Ft. Lauderdale, Florida, teen says, "I knew that there would be nothing funny or exciting about a pig being flung into a crowd of gawking teenagers with loud music, cheers, and bright lights."

He asked friends to write letters protesting the idea, and he submitted them to the school administration. A few days before the contest, Michael learned that the school had switched to a fake pig instead: a teacher dressed in a pig costume! "Using this more humorous alternative was, in my opinion, funnier and much more worthwhile!" Michael says.

Eryn hoped to volunteer at the animal shelter near her Omaha, Nebraska, home, but its rules said a volunteer had to be at least 15 years old. So the middle school student came up with an innovative way to assist animals in need. Eryn wrote columns about shelter animals in the "Voice for Teens" page of Omaha's *Morning World-Herald* newspaper. What a novel idea!

Gabriel also put his pen to work to help animals. When the Westchester, New York, boy was 8 years old, his two pet hamsters died from old age. "I was very sad," he remembers. "I imagined a special place they went to called Hamster Dam, and I wrote about it. It made me feel better to think of them in such a wonderful and happy place."

Gabriel spent two years writing and illustrating his healing book, *Hamster Dam*. According to Gabriel, hamsters are "furry and little and lovable and have their own personality. Some of them are really nice, and some aren't."

Gabriel donates half of the profits from his book to his favorite charity: Green Chimneys. It's a farm where kids can learn about themselves by interacting with animals. He describes it as "a place for animals and children that helps not one but both of them, and they get along together."

Troubled Kids Work with Animals

For 60 years Green Chimneys, a special education school in Brewster, New York, has been pairing troubled kids with animals. This partnership has transformed the lives of students with emotional, behavioral, and learning challenges. Animal-assisted therapy creates brighter futures for both people and animals.

The campus is home to more than 300 animals who teach kids animal awareness. The kids can help care for injured or orphaned birds of prey and other wildlife at the rehabilitation center. They can rehabilitate farm animals such as Dottie, a Yorkshire pig who had been kept in a Bronx apartment.

Or they can prepare Golden Retrievers to become service dogs, assisting people in wheelchairs. Students work with East Coast Assistance Dogs to train puppies. They use positive rewards to teach the dogs how to turn on light switches and take food out of the refrigerator.

Sara, 15, helped train some of the more than 30 service dogs placed across the country. As a result of working with the dogs she says, "I accomplished something most people in life never accomplish—I changed my life." It's a win-win situation. As they learn about the harmonious relationship between people and animals, these kids regain a sense of self-worth.

Another program, k9 connection, also pairs troubled kids with homeless dogs, leading to success stories on both sides. It matches 12- to 18-year-old at-risk kids with shelter dogs, creating a training partnership. The Santa Monica, California, organization was started in 2005 by Katherine Beattie and Patricia Sinclair.

Both the dogs and their teenage trainers learn valuable lessons when they participate in the three-week k9 connection program. First, students are matched with homeless shelter dogs. Since both have experienced being unwanted, they form strong bonds.

Then students transform themselves into trainers. They learn how to use positive reinforcement (praising and rewarding good behavior) to teach basic obedience skills that will make the dogs more adoptable. Students spend two hours each day teaching dogs to sit, stay, and walk on a leash without tugging.

While the dogs gain confidence and show off their new skills, their trainers acquire "patience, compassion, and responsibility," according to Katherine. Along with the dogs, these teenage trainers also learn the power of positive reinforcement. They can apply the lessons to their own lives as an alternative to at-risk behaviors such as fighting.

The magical connection that forms between dogs and teens can be seen at the graduation ceremony. Pooches show off their new skills along with a few tricks, and then head off to their new homes. Their proud trainers continue a relationship with k9 connection, with some returning as interns.

An Experiment in Combating Cruelty

Rory, from the Australian Science and Mathematics School in Adelaide, challenged the myth that goldfish have only a three-second memory. His motivation? Rory wanted to show that it's cruel to keep goldfish in tiny tanks.

"We are told that a goldfish has a memory span of less than three seconds and that no matter how small its tank is, it will always discover new places and objects," the teen says. "I wanted to challenge this theory, as I believe it is a myth intended to make us feel less guilty about keeping fish in small tanks."

Rory spent three weeks training his goldfish to swim to a light to get his fish food. Once his goldfish reduced the time to reach the light from one minute to less than five seconds, Rory removed the light.

Six days later, he replaced the light. Again, his goldfish swam to it in less than five seconds. Obviously, the fish remembered the link between the light and food.

"My results strongly showed that goldfish can retain knowledge for at least six days. They can retain that knowledge indefinitely if they use it regularly," says Rory.

Things You Can Do Today to Make a Difference

- Create a brochure or newsletter about local animal welfare issues and share it with your community.

- Spread the word. Write a report, give a speech, draw a picture, or sing a song about an animal topic that you feel passionate about. Create T-shirts with animal messages and logos for friends and classmates. Enlighten your friends, family, classmates, and teachers.

- If you attend a school in California, Florida, Illinois, Louisiana, Maine, Maryland, Massachusetts, New Jersey, New Mexico, New York, Oregon, Pennsylvania, Rhode Island, Vermont, or Virginia, you have the right to choose a nonanimal alternative to dissection. No matter what state you live in, you can still ask your school to offer nonanimal alternatives to dissection.

- Write a letter to the editor of a newspaper or magazine explaining why a particular animal issue is important to you. Or make a phone call to a radio or television station requesting more coverage of animal topics.

- Team up with others to pick up litter at the beach, especially plastic bags. Sea turtles mistake this trash for jellyfish and eat it. When a turtle eats a bag, the plastic blocks the turtle's stomach and causes starvation. Ask local businesses to sponsor your group by donating garbage bags and lunch.

- Never buy any products made from sea turtles, including tortoiseshell jewelry and combs. Many of these creatures are killed as they return to sea, when they are defenseless after laying their eggs.

All Creatures
Great and Small

Kids have extended the circle of compassion to enrich the lives of wild and endangered animals. They are willing to raise their voices for those who cannot speak for themselves, protecting animals and the habitats in which they live.

Saving One Animal at a Time

A drama unfolded at Lake Hogan in Valley Springs, California, when a pair of dogs chased three deer off an island in the lake. The two does and a fawn jumped into the water and paddled toward the mainland, about a half a mile away.

Sarah had been waterskiing with her parents. Together they pulled the dogs on board their boat so they could return the dogs to their people, who were also waterskiing.

Suddenly, the young fawn started desperately paddling in circles and sinking below the surface. Sarah jumped onto a large water tube that her parents pulled behind their boat. Then they zoomed across the lake toward the fawn. The young woman dove off the tube and grabbed the fawn in a dramatic rescue.

"I have always been an animal lover, so there was no hesitation in my decision to save the fawn," Sarah recalls. Another boat retrieved the heroine and the fawn. Sarah and her parents released the fawn where they had seen the two does swim ashore. Then they shoved off to watch the happy reunion from a distance.

Sarah has rescued other creatures, including a 2-week-old Chihuahua and a duck. She is currently in the Exotic Animal Training and Management Program at Moorpark College in California. Sarah plans to continue her "passion for nature through the development of a wildlife outreach program that will educate the next generation of children about the environment and wildlife, hopefully to inspire others to help make a difference."

On Mother's Day, two teens were rushing home in a downpour after buying bouquets for their moms when they saw a frantic duck and heard chirping. Adrian, 14, and Adam, 13, followed the chirps and discovered that a flock of ducklings had become trapped in a storm sewer that was blocked by a heavy manhole cover.

The Milwaukee, Wisconsin, boys flagged down a police officer, and together they managed to pry off the lid. Then Adrian and Adam took turns holding each other's ankles and grabbing the ducklings out of the sewer. The boys saved all the ducks, who were later released at a park. What a grand Mother's Day present for the mother duck!

When Guy found a helpless baby bird on the sidewalk near his house on Staten Island in New York City, his first reaction was, "I have to protect him!" So Guy, 13, searched for the baby bird's nest and the parents.

When he couldn't find either, he contacted a wildlife rehabilitator, who explained how to care for the bird until he was ready to fly away. Guy fed the tiny bird round the clock. "He was so cute, I wished I wouldn't have to let him go some day," Guy recalls. But he knew that wild animals can never live happily inside our homes.

Eight days later it was time to let the baby bird fly free. Guy continues to look for him every day in the neighborhood trees.

"I'm proud that I could help that bird," he says, "but I did learn that in the future, if a baby bird is out of his nest and in a safe location, it's best not to touch him because his parents will most likely continue feeding him on the ground."

Taking on the Circus

Circuses aren't fun for elephants and other animals.

Alexandra, 7, wore an elephant mask and a T-shirt that said "Vote Yes" when she threw out the ceremonial first pitch at a Chicago Cubs baseball game. She hoped the sold-out crowd would support the Elephant Protection Ordinance.

This landmark elephant protection law would ban the use of chains, electric prods, and bull hooks on these sensitive beasts. It would also ensure that any elephant brought into Chicago would have room to roam.

Alexandra won the opportunity to throw the pitch thanks to an online charity auction. She spent her summer gathering signatures in support of the ordinance.

When Andrew was only 4, he proudly addressed a crowd gathered at an anti-circus protest. The young boy grabbed the microphone and said, "Animals should not be in circuses. They should be home with their families, like me." A sponsor of the circus pulled aside Andrew's mother, Lydia, and told her this was the one comment he'd heard that made sense to him. And the circus did not go forward that year.

Now Andrew extends his compassion to domestic and farm creatures. Each year, he donates his birthday money to an animal charity such as Farm Sanctuary or Cat Assistance, where he adopted two of his cats.

Picking Up the Garbage

The *Guinness World Records* book called California Coastal Cleanup Day "the largest garbage collection." Tens of thousands of volunteers collected hundreds of thousands of pounds of trash, making the coastline safer for sea creatures.

Every September, volunteers across California join together on Coastal Cleanup Day to remove garbage from shorelines and the sea. In 2007, more than 60,000 volunteers worked hard to collect more than 900,000 pounds of trash and recyclables.

One young volunteer, Erin, age 7, explained why she spent her day picking up trash. "It's important to clean our shorelines because marine animals can get hurt and sick from trash that ends up in the water. Sea turtles get their heads and legs stuck in string and trash. Otters and seabirds get tangled up in six-pack soda rings. When plastic bags fill up with water and float around, they look like jellyfish. Sea animals sometimes think these plastic bags are food and swallow them. This makes their stomachs feel full, so they don't eat real food. They can starve," she says.

When Erin joined her mother at Ocean Beach in San Francisco, she found "Styrofoam, pieces of plastic, plastic bags, soda cans, nails, and about 150 cigarette butts." She urges people to "go to the beach any day, not just on Coastal Cleanup Day, and pick up trash. Trash can really mess up the environment."

You can also adopt a local lake, river, or stream to clean. The creatures who live there will thank you for helping to keep their home safe for them.

Saving Wild Habitats

One of the biggest threats wild animals face is loss of habitat—having no place safe and clean to live and breed. So saving habitat is an important part of saving wildlife.

Three seventh-grade students from Hawken Upper School in Gates Mills, Ohio, wanted to do something locally that was related to both the environment and wildlife. The girls—Evin, Angela, and Amanda—tested the water quality of streams in their region. They determined that pollution was having a negative effect on the threatened native Ohio brook trout.

"Brookies," who live in streams, lakes, and ponds and are speckled with ruby spots, "really needed a voice," says Evin. The girls founded Save Our Stream (SOS) in 2002 to preserve the trout's habitat and educate local residents about the threatened fish.

Evin recalls, "When we started SOS in middle school, we got a lot of weird looks and comments from people. 'You want to do what?' they'd say. Socially, middle school is a jungle, but it didn't faze me."

The girls stuck to it and received more than $38,000 in grants and awards. They used the money to educate their community "in an attempt to reduce environmental degradation, raise awareness, and promote conscientious land stewardship," according to Evin. They've rehabilitated damaged streams, designed educational trail signs for parks, made presentations to classrooms, and organized river restoration projects.

As Save Our Stream improved the brook trout's fragile environment, the fish population began to grow in their region. "The brook trout is the poster child for everything I'm fighting for," Evin says.

Grace was only 5 when she realized that small gestures could be of big importance to animals. She visited an animal shelter to help her mother and sister, Hannah, adopt a cat. Grace decided to donate to the shelter the $25 she had received as a Christmas gift.

A Christmas present of a stuffed manatee prompted the Deposit, New York, girl to learn more about the creatures. She visited Save the Manatee Club's web site and became determined to help these marine mammals.

"I care for animals," says Grace. "The manatees are losing their habitat and getting hurt by motorboats. I want to do whatever I can to help them survive."

Grace set up a lemonade stand on a rainy summer day. Despite the weather, she hoped to raise enough money to adopt one manatee. Of course this manatee would not be living in Grace's bathtub! When you "adopt" one, you receive a photo and biography of the manatee you select, along with the knowledge that your adoption fee will help protect endangered manatees. At the end of the day, her persistence paid off. Grace was able to adopt three manatees.

Since then she has adopted a dozen more. Grace raised more money selling hot cocoa and cookies during a Christmas parade. She received donations after being featured in her local paper. Everywhere she goes, Grace informs people about the difficulties manatees face. She's gearing up to sell lemonade again this summer, with a goal of selling enough to adopt five more manatees.

Hands-on with Wildlife

Amanda can be found most summer days at PAWS Wildlife Rehabilitation Center in Lynnwood, Washington. The teen may be preparing meals for the animals, hand-feeding baby songbirds and mammals, or assisting wildlife rehabilitators and veterinarians with medical care. Or she may be performing less glamorous but necessary jobs such as scrubbing cages or doing laundry.

She's already logged 350 hours, frequently arriving at eight in the morning and staying until ten at night. She was named Wildlife Care Assistant Volunteer of the Year for 2005 and has earned the gratitude of the more than 200 species that the wildlife center cares for.

Budding biologists are also working with wildlife in Puerto Rico to save the crested toad from extinction.

One good thing came out of the hurricane that ripped through the island of Puerto Rico in 1998. The Puerto Rican crested toad came out to breed in ponds that formed after Hurricane Georges' heavy rainfall. These warty toads with golden eyes and upturned snouts are threatened by habitat loss—having no more wild places where they can live. Species that were introduced onto the island by humans, such as the mongoose and rat, also cause trouble because they eat the toads.

Many Puerto Ricans weren't even aware that the crested toad existed. The creatures are small, only three or four inches long, and are active only at night. The only spot on Earth where the toads lived in the wild was in a sandy shallow pond in the northern town of Quebradillas. And until the crested toads were spotted there after the hurricane, the pond was being used as a parking lot!

An 11th-grade science class spread across the town to search for the toads. The group of 15, concerned about the threatened species, formed Students for the Conservation of the Puerto Rican Crested Toad. These conservation-minded kids conducted fieldwork by searching for the rare toads in their wild habitat along the rocky coasts. The students also checked out ponds for tadpoles. They kept their eyes open for other amphibians, such as the larger common toad, who could compete for food and space. The data the students collected helped scientists determine if competition poses a threat to the crested toad.

"I like this kind of biology work," says Alcides, 17. "I'm helping protect the species of my town."

Making Zoos Better for the Animals

Beau, a Masai giraffe at Franklin Park Zoo in Boston, suffered from a terrible disease. The 16-foot-tall giraffe had lost 300 pounds. He needed a special diet consisting of 50 pounds of fresh leaves, branches, and vegetables each day. Beau's expensive meals would cost $50,000 per year.

Autumn, 9, learned about Beau's fate when she saw him on the television news. The Pelham, New Hampshire, girl collected coins and soda cans, donated her allowance and birthday money, and asked her parents to set up a collection can for the ailing giraffe in their convenience store.

Autumn collected more than $7,000 for Beau's special diet. Not only did the giraffe regain the weight, but he also became a proud father in January 2006. His mate, Jana, had a healthy baby female giraffe. Zoo caretakers gave the baby the perfect name: Autumn.

Justin, 13, of Elk Grove, California, got the nickname Bear Boy for his efforts to relocate a pair of bears. Ursula and Brutus are California black bears who had spent their lives in a bare steel cage after the Roseville town zoo closed. The stressed-out bears paced their cage endlessly, wearing a path in the concrete floor.

"It's just a bad situation for any animal to live in," Justin says. He spent every day for three years raising money to help move the 20-year-old bears to the nearby Folsom Zoo, which built a new, enriched habitat for them. He raised $25,000!

In the past, children were encouraged to donate coins to help zoos buy elephants. In 1955, kids broke their piggy banks and sent in pennies to purchase Penny, an African elephant who lived at the San Francisco Zoo for 40 years.

More modern kids at the Crossroads and New Roads private schools in Santa Monica, California, confronted the Los Angeles Board of Zoo Commissioners in 1998. The students urged that the four elephants living in the Los Angeles Zoo pack up their trunks and retire to the Elephant Sanctuary in Hohenwald, Tennessee, instead of living sad lives in concrete and steel enclosures. One lucky African elephant from the zoo, Ruby, was eventually retired in 2007 at the age of 45 to the Performing Animal Welfare Society Wildlife Sanctuary in San Andreas, California.

Protecting the Rain Forest

Back in 1987 in a rural Swedish school, Roland, 9, and his class studied tropical rain forests and the amazing animals who live there.

The boy wondered how students could protect the special creatures and their home. Roland's class learned about a forest in a mountain range of northwestern Costa Rica. This tropical region contained an evergreen forest, a cloud forest, and a rain forest. All were in danger of disappearing because humans wanted to clear the natural landscape.

Roland and his class decided to save a small section of the rain forest so no one could cut down trees for farms, pastures, cities, and roads. The students raised $1,500, which was enough to buy about 15 acres of land. Guided by scientists and conservationists from the Monteverde Conservation League, Roland and his class formed the Children's Eternal Rain Forest.

Students from all around the globe joined in with innovative ideas to raise funds. Some built a miniature rain forest and held guided tours. Others hosted plant-a-thons and cleanups in local parks, held walk-a-thons to parks and reserves, and sold greenery through adopt-a-tree programs. This international group of kids has raised enough money to buy 54,000 acres, making their rain forest the largest private reserve in Costa Rica!

The Children's Eternal Rain Forest shelters spectacular species. More than 400 different birds, including the exotic Resplendent Quetzal, flock there. Visitors can see many mammals such as sloths, coatimundis, hog-nosed skunks, armadillos, and monkeys. Iguanas, lizards, frogs, and snakes slither, hop, and sun in the rain forest. Butterflies and bats swoop through the air. All are safe, thanks to children around the world.

Phebe, 17, wanted to make the world a better place through volunteer service. The Vermont teen gathered together an energetic bunch of middle school and high school students and formed Change the World Kids. Phebe believes that "no one can do everything, but everybody can do something." That something focuses on saving the bellbird and other endangered animals in the Costa Rican rain forest. Due to a loss of habitat, these creatures could disappear. When people cut down the rain forests, the fruit trees that birds and animals depend on for their food vanish.

Together with Costa Rican biologists and conservationists, Change the World Kids established *Bosque para Siempre*, the Forever Forest. The kids held fund-raisers, selling Costa Rican coffee (shade grown to help sustain rain forests and provide bird habitats) and tickets to dinner parties featuring talks by rain-forest experts. With the more than $150,000 these determined students raised, they purchased parcels of land to create an area where migrating rain-forest birds and animals will always be safe and able to find food. Change the World Kids hopes to eventually protect a 300-hectare corridor, which they think will cost $1.8 million.

Phebe hopes to motivate kids around the world to save this rain-forest habitat, where many endangered species live. "The work and motivation to make the world a better place don't happen miraculously," she says. "Those things really come from the heart."

Evan also became a champion for the rain forests to protect "the homes of jaguars, spider monkeys, orchids, sea turtles, and thousands of butterflies." At the age of 3, the future environmentalist told his mother, "I want to be rich so I can buy all the land so no one can build houses on it and take the homes away from the animals."

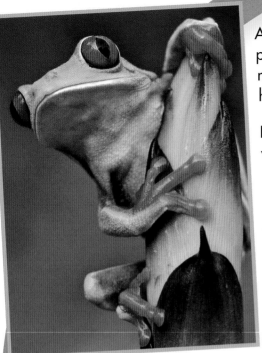

At 7, Evan formed the Red Dragon Conservation Team to purchase and protect Costa Rican rain forests. The team raises funds during an annual bowl-a-thon. Together, they have purchased more than 16 acres of threatened habitat.

Evan reaches out to other conservation-minded kids via his web site. He reminds them that "every little bit counts."

Five-year-old Connor adores amphibians. "I like frogs because they can jump really high," the boy explains, adding that he wants to be a "frog saver" when he grows up.

Connor became concerned when he learned that his favorite frog—the red-eyed treefrog—was at risk. This amphibian's rain-forest home is under constant threat as people clear the land to grow crops.

Connor's sister, Kaley, 7, came up with the idea of throwing a "froggy party" to raise money for the Rainforest Alliance. "I just knew that a lot of animals lived in the rainforest, so if I saved acres of it, it would really help lots of animals. I had the idea that a party would get lots of people to come, but also donate their spare change," she said.

The two kids planned the party at their Bellevue, Washington, home. "We put facts about the rain forest up on our walls so people would know what they were saving," Kaley explains. "We also put on a rain-forest movie, got rain-forest books from the library, and put out rain-forest coloring pages. I think we really encouraged the people at the party to keep donating."

Together, the brother and sister team raised almost $800—enough to save 16 acres of rain forest. "I felt very good after the party because I think we saved a lot of animals," says Kaley, who is planning a coral reef party next. Her brother adds, "The party was really cool. I wish it could've gone on forever."

No More Turtle Races

lex befriended a wild turtle he named Minn, whom he discovered in a dry creek bed near his southeastern Missouri home. "She never turned down the treats I offered," Alex recalls. That is, until the teen entered Minn in a turtle race.

In this county fair event, a group of turtles compete to see which one will be the first to race out of a circle drawn on the ground. Since a large number of turtle contestants usually race throughout the day, elimination races are held. The winning turtles then race against each other until the overall winner is declared.

However, Minn was not destined to be in the winner's circle. "During the race, Minn refused all the treats I offered her, and she seemed to be upset," Alex says. "I released Minn in the exact spot where I found her, but I felt bad for what I put her through."

Curious about Minn's negative reaction, Alex researched turtle racing to try to determine why it isn't fun for the contestants. He discovered that these races are harmful to turtles.

According to Alex, "Box turtles are sensitive to their environment and need specially arranged enclosures and diets. Without these, they often become sick, developing diseases such as pneumonia and shell rot. Unfortunately, most people collecting turtles for races are either not aware or not concerned about these possibilities."

Another serious problem occurs when wild turtles are captured for racing, resulting in a decline in wild populations. "Box turtles have low fecundity, meaning that they have few offspring, but long life spans, sometimes over a century," Alex explains. "In many turtle populations, we see a delicate balance where slight increases in mortality or collection can cause declines. The turtles just don't reproduce fast enough to replace themselves in these situations."

Alex attended turtle races in four different states and researched turtle racing around the country. He found that an average of 65 turtles entered each race, and then estimated that about 27,000 box turtles race annually.

"This level of collection could potentially devastate box turtle populations. It is particularly disconcerting when you consider that over 500,000 box turtles will be used if things continue at this rate for the next 20 years," Alex says.

He presented his findings at the Box Turtle Conservation Workshop to explain how racing stresses turtle populations. Alex hopes to get a degree in wildlife ecology to continue championing the cause of box turtles.

Sticking Up for Primates

Washo grew up in Oregon with a menagerie of rescued pets. The Native American teen has a particular passion for primates. He became motivated to start an enrichment program for monkeys at the Oregon National Primate Research Center after watching protesters outside the research facility.

Washo arranged a meeting with the director of the center and proposed his idea to improve living conditions for the monkeys. The teen began three Roots & Shoots programs for the primates, each geared toward different grade levels: elementary school, middle school, and high school.

Roots & Shoots, a program of the Jane Goodall Institute, believes that "the power of youth is global." The network branches out to tens of thousands of kids in nearly 100 countries to inspire positive change for animals and their environments.

Washo led the Oregon Roots & Shoots kids in fun projects such as making monkey treats, creating interactive food toys, and designing ladders. The research center invited the kids to their site so they could transplant bamboo into containers near the monkey enclosures.

Word of Washo's work spread, and next he helped with the chimpanzee exhibit at the Oregon Zoo. The animal lover became a ZooTeen volunteer and then an intern in the primate department.

"This experience has taught me not to give up on something I believe in just because of my age or because I am only one person," says Washo. "Seeing what we're accomplishing makes me realize that if you just get involved, you can change the world."

In another Jane Goodall Institute project, hundreds of kids across the country came up with creative fund-raising campaigns to raise $40,000 for orphan chimpanzees at the Tchimpounga Chimpanzee Rehabilitation Center. This orphanage, created by the Jane Goodall Institute in the Congo Basin, is Africa's largest ape sanctuary. The money will build a new dormitory for orphaned baby chimps, whose families were killed for bushmeat (flesh from African wildlife, including primates and elephants).

An impressive range of ideas brought in the big bucks. Third graders from the Larchmont Charter School in Los Angeles raised $430 by selling more than 50 handmade necklaces. In Salt Lake City, Utah, two students hosted a pet show in the park, earning more than $450. New York members of Roots & Shoots read chimp-themed books at a local library and played a Barrel of Monkeys game to gather donations.

Eight-year-old Brandon gave presentations at Eastern Illinois University. The Charleston, Illinois, boy was motivated by the idea of helping chimp babies have a second chance at life. He dressed in a safari outfit and passed around a donation jar for "chimp change," collecting $319. "I wanted to raise a hundred million dollars at first," says Brandon. "In a perfect world, there would be no habitat destruction and everyone would treat animals the way they would want to be treated."

Other kids sold fruits and vegetables they raised at a community farmer's market, designed and sold T-shirts, and collected change instead of candy while trick-or-treating. Thanks to all these big-hearted kids, change for the chimps is possible.

Learning to Live Together

Four students at Birch Lane Elementary School in Massapequa Park, New York, accepted a challenge from their science teacher. How could they remove the droppings that a gaggle of 100 geese deposited on local grasslands? "Every time we'd go outside for recess or gym, the field was covered with goose poop, and we'd track it all through school and it would even get into our stuff," says Arielle.

Arielle and her friends Cassandra, Grace, and Nicolette tackled the poop problem with their invention, the Pooper Scooper Plow 2000. The plow, which looks like a box on wheels, scoops up poop and deposits it into a trash bag. The four friends won praise for their humane solution from Wildlife Watch and the Coalition to Prevent the Destruction of Canada Geese.

"We realized we were never going to eliminate the geese, and we didn't want to kill them," Arielle says. "I mean, everyone does it—you know, poops. You shouldn't be killed for something like that."

The sixth graders were finalists for the Christopher Columbus Fellowship Foundation Award, a national competition for students who have devised solutions to local problems. Go Team Pooper Scooper!

Flocks of trumpeter swans congregate around Jackson Hole, Wyoming, in the winter. There, fog rises off of Flat Creek, making it difficult sometimes for the swans to see. Each year, some of these threatened birds collide with electric power lines.

When Nicole was 8, she discovered a dead trumpeter swan near an area with power lines. The girl started Save the Swans campaign to protect the majestic birds. She spent two years raising $12,000 toward getting trenches dug and power lines buried.

In 2002, Nicole accomplished her goal of burying a one-mile stretch. Thanks to her, a dramatic reduction in swan fatalities was observed in the Flat Creek region.

A group of fifth graders from Oakland Terrace Elementary School in Panama City, Florida, got a lesson in how government works when they voiced their concerns about local beaver colonies.

Beavers are nature's conservationists. When they dam small streams, they create ponds that hold large amounts of water. The water flows slowly, preventing flooding and soil erosion. However, when these large rodents build in constructed drainage areas, conflicts arise.

Nena led the students in their quest to find a way to curb beaver damage without harming the creatures. She started a petition at her school to propose alternatives to removing or killing the "problem" beavers. Nena knew that beavers bring many benefits when they create wetlands, and that coexisting is the best solution.

The students researched humane alternatives. They proposed solutions such as tree guards made of wire cylinders and beaver baffles that control objectionable flooding through pipes. By suggesting plans of action rather than just complaining, students learned to position themselves for success.

Things You Can Do Today to Make a Difference

- Do not participate in or attend turtle races. Explain to others why these events are inhumane.

- Leave wild turtles where you find them. Turtles, particularly those who are caught in the wild, do not make good pets because they are difficult to care for in captivity.

- Hold a rain-forest-themed dance as a fund-raiser. Decorate the school gymnasium to resemble a colorful tropical forest, complete with pictures and posters of exotic amphibians, birds, insects, mammals, and plants, and maybe an assortment of exotic stuffed toys. Don't forget to play a mix of global music to represent rain forests around the world. Serve rain-forest foods such as chocolate, papayas, nuts, and bananas. Sell handmade environmental gifts like note cards and T-shirts.

- "Adopt" a wild or endangered animal (such as a manatee) from an organization that protects both the creatures and their habitat. You can split the annual membership cost with a friend.

- Contact sponsors of circuses, rodeos, box turtle races, and other events that use animals for entertainment. Explain why these events are not entertaining for the animals and that you will be boycotting them. Suggest that the sponsors support a more humane form of entertainment. As more and more kids refuse to buy tickets to entertainment events that use animals, they will eventually stop.

Resources

Here's a list of the organizations that help animals that were mentioned in this book. Pick one, or choose one near your home, and check out its web site for volunteer opportunities.

Amaryllis Farm Equine Rescue
www.forrascal.com
This rescue farm with locations throughout the east end of Long Island saves horses and ponies who are on their way to the slaughterhouse and helps them find new homes.

Animal Rights Community of Greater Cincinnati
www.greenpeople.org
This Ohio group works to educate the public about how animals are used and abused for fur, food, entertainment, and research.

ASPCA
www.aspca.org
Founded in 1866 to prevent the cruelty animals faced then, this national group continues to battle abuse and work for the well-being of animals today.

Associated Humane Society of New Jersey
ahscares.org
This is a group of three animal shelters and Popcorn Park Zoo, a place for abandoned, injured, ill, exploited, abused, and very old wildlife, exotic animals, farm animals, and birds.

Augies Doggies Rescue
members.petfinder.com/~PA394
This all-breed dog rescue near Chicago saves the lives of animals who would otherwise be killed in animal shelters.

Best Friends Animal Society
www.bestfriends.org
A sanctuary in southern Utah, this organization offers a home to about 2,000 dogs, cats, and other creatures arriving from shelters and rescue groups around the country to get special care.

Brooklyn Children's Museum

www.brooklynkids.org

The first museum created just for children when it was founded in 1899, this New York museum features hands-on exhibits that are fun and educational.

California Coastal Cleanup Day

www.coastal.ca.gov/publiced/ccd/ccd.html

This volunteer event focuses on the ocean environment, where more than 800,000 Californians have removed 12 million pounds of trash from beaches.

Cat Assistance

www.petfinder.com/shelters/NY24.html

This small private cat shelter in New York City rescues cats and kittens from both private owners who are forced to give up their pets and from the Center for Animal Care and Control, which is the official city shelter.

Cathy's Rottie Rescue Rehab and Sanctuary

www.petfinder.com/shelters/cathysrottie

This Connecticut group is dedicated to the rescue of abandoned, abused, and neglected Rottweilers, with the goal of finding permanent, loving homes for the dogs.

Change the World Kids

changetheworldkids.org

These students, based in Vermont, are dedicated to making the world a better place by helping individuals in their community and organizations and environments worldwide.

Children's Eternal Rain Forest

www.childrenseternalrainforest.com

This 54,000-acre rain forest in northwestern Costa Rica is paid for by kids' contributions. It is home to 60 species of amphibians, 101 types of reptiles, 425 kinds of birds, and 121 species of mammals.

Coalition to Prevent the Destruction of Canada Geese

www.canadageese.org

This wildlife protection organization in New York specializes in helping Canada Geese.

Crosses 4 Critters

www.morningstarcorona.org/critters.htm
This children's ministry in California raises money to help people with limited income provide veterinary care for their animals.

Dalhart Animal Wellness Group and Sanctuary (DAWGS)

www.dawgsntexas.com
This Texas sanctuary has rescued more than 3,900 animals and continues to work to make a difference in their community.

Dearborn Animal Shelter

www.dearborn-animals.com
This Michigan shelter cares for more than 2,500 animals each year.

Earth Island Institute

www.earthisland.org
This California organization supports people dedicated to conserving, preserving, and restoring the ecosystems on which our civilization depends.

East Coast Assistance Dogs

www.ecad1.org
This Dobbs Ferry, New York, group trains dogs to help people with disabilities.

The Elephant Sanctuary

www.elephants.com
Operating on 2,700 acres in Tennessee, this is the nation's largest natural habitat refuge developed specifically for endangered African and Asian elephants.

EmanciPET

www.emancipet.org
This Texas organization prevents animal homelessness and death by providing low-cost or free spay and neuter of dogs and cats.

Farm Sanctuary

www.farmsanctuary.org
These 175-acre New York and 300-acre California farms work to end

cruelty to farm animals and promote compassionate living through rescue, education, and advocacy.

Friends of County Animal Shelters

www.focas.us
This corporation supports the Bergen County Animal Shelter in New Jersey by promoting the general welfare and natural conservation, preservation, and protection of all animals.

Friends of the Fairmont Animal Shelter

fofas.org
This animal rescue organization is dedicated to the rescue, foster, and adoption of companion animals in California.

Furry Friends Network

www.furryfriendsnetwork.com
This rescue group in central Pennsylvania places homeless animals in foster homes until they can be adopted.

Green Chimneys

www.greenchimneys.org
This 166-acre New York farm has a special school where nearly 200 students with emotional, behavioral, and learning challenges care for and interact with the farm's rescued livestock and wildlife.

Hawaiian Humane Society

www.hawaiianhumane.org
In Honolulu, this society serves as a shelter for homeless animals, a rescue operation, a placement agency, and an educational and advocacy organization.

Heartland Rabbit Rescue

www.heartlandrabbitrescue.org
This shelter in Oklahoma is devoted to rescuing and caring for abandoned and neglected domestic rabbits.

Heart of the Catskills Humane Society

www.heartofthecatskills.org
This small rural animal shelter with a mighty heart in the Catskill Mountains

of New York tries to match every adoptable pet with a loving home.

House Rabbit Society
www.rabbit.org
This national organization with 30 local chapters is dedicated to rescuing and rehoming abandoned domestic rabbits and educating the public about rabbit care.

Humane Animal Welfare Society
www.hawspets.org
This Wisconsin shelter helps more than 6,000 animals each year and promotes the humane care and treatment of all animals.

Humane Society of Central Oregon
www.hsco.org
This Bend, Oregon, society has animals available for adoption and also sponsors community education and fundraising events.

Humane Society of Southwestern Michigan
www.humanesocietyswm.org
This Benton Harbor, Michigan, organization provides shelter and care to sick, homeless, abused, and unwanted animals.

Ian's Bead Company
www.iansbeadcompany.com
This community service crafts project is formed by kids in the Chicago region to benefit homeless dogs.

k9 connection
www.k9connection.org
This project educates, counsels, and inspires at-risk youth by teaching them how to help homeless shelter dogs.

Labs4Rescue
labs4rescue.com
This all-volunteer organization in Connecticut is dedicated to providing a new life for rescued or homeless Labrador Retrievers and Labrador mixes.

Last Hope, Inc.

www.last-hope.org
This network of foster homes in Minnesota saves abandoned, unwanted dogs and cats.

Little Shelter Animal Rescue & Adoption Center

www.littleshelter.com
This Long Island shelter is dedicated to saving all companion animals whose lives are in danger.

Lucky Paws Rabbit Rescue

luckypawsrabbitrescue.org
This central New York group of volunteers rescues abandoned rabbits, spays or neuters them, and then finds permanent homes.

Maine Vest-a-Dog

mainevestadog.homestead.com
This foundation is dedicated to protecting Maine's police dogs with bulletproof and stab-proof vests.

Mollywood Parrot Rescue and Sanctuary

www.mollywood.org
This Washington bird sanctuary provides a permanent, safe, and loving home for parrots.

Montville Pet Parents

www.montvillepetparents.org
This New Jersey volunteer group is committed to building a kinder world for homeless pets by raising money to build a new shelter.

A New Leash on Life

nlol.org/Chicago
This Chicago organization is committed to finding loving homes for shelter dogs who might otherwise be killed because they have no home.

PAWS

www.paws.org
Based in Washington State, the Progressive Animal Welfare Society shelters homeless animals and rehabilitates injured and orphaned wildlife.

Performing Animal Welfare Society Wildlife Sanctuary

www.pawsweb.org/paws_wildlife_ sanctuaries_home_page.html
This sanctuary in California is a place where abandoned or abused performing and exotic animals can live in peace.

Rabbit March

www.rabbitmatch.org
This Los Angeles group finds permanent indoor homes for abandoned house rabbits.

Rainforest Alliance

www.rainforest-alliance.org
Based in New York, the alliance works with people whose livelihoods depend on the rain forest, helping them transform the way they grow food, harvest wood, and host travelers.

Red Dragons Conservation Team

rdct.org
This is an international group of kids who are taking action to take better care of the Earth.

The Rescue House

www.rescuehouse.org
This cat rescue organization in California finds loving homes for unwanted, abandoned, homeless, and abused cats.

Roots & Shoots

www.rootsandshoots.org
This network of tens of thousands of young people in almost 100 countries connects youth of all ages who share a common desire to help make our world a better place.

Save the Manatee Club

www.savethemanatee.org
Based in Florida, this national organization strives to protect manatees and their watery habitats for future generations.

The Smile Retrievers

www.thesmileretrievers.com

These therapy dogs from Staten Island, New York, are trained to help people who face a crisis to cope with their grief.

Staten Island Children's Museum

statenislandkids.org

Twice a year, this New York City institution hosts the ASPCA Mini-Camp for Kids. It also offers other animal-themed experiences.

Teens Against Whaling

www.teensagainstwhaling.com

This Australian conservation group is determined to create awareness and bring a stop to whale hunting.

Town Lake Animal Center

www.ci.austin.tx.us/animals/

The largest animal shelter in central Texas provides a safe haven to more than 23,000 animals each year.

Valley Animal Center

www.valleyanimal.org

This is a community-supported shelter for dogs and cats in California.

Vest-A-Dog

www.vestadog.com

This nationwide foundation is committed to providing bulletproof vests to law enforcement dogs throughout the country.

Wildlife Watch

www.wildwatch.org

This New York group combines education, political awareness, and direct aid to help protect individual wild animals and species.

Wyatt's Ruff Rescues

www.petfinder.com/shelters/ wyattsruffrescues.html

This small central Florida rescue group saves dogs scheduled to be killed in shelters, spays or neuters them, and offers them for adoption.

About the Authors

Nancy Furstinger

Nancy Furstinger has been speaking up for animals since she learned to talk—and she hasn't shut up yet. Nancy volunteers for an assortment of humane societies and rescue groups, and she has been a vegetarian since the age of 16. She's flunked "Fostering 101" many times with her trio of rescued pooches and seven house rabbits. Nancy has been a feature writer for a daily newspaper, a managing editor of trade and consumer magazines, and an editor at two children's book publishers. She is also the author of more than 100 books, including many on her favorite topic: animals! Nancy was born on April 10—ASPCA day.

Dr. Sheryl L. Pipe

Sheryl L. Pipe, PhD, is the senior director of humane education at the ASPCA. In this position she writes articles and the curriculum for courses, presents workshops at local and national conferences, initiates projects, and oversees the work of a department of seven talented staff members. Sheryl has had companion animals her entire life. She lives in New Jersey with her husband, David, a son, Joshua, a dog named Bailey, and cats from A to Z: Alex, Maxine, Moshe, Samantha, and Zachary.

About the ASPCA

The American Society for the Prevention of Cruelty to Animals (ASPCA) was founded in 1866 by a wealthy man from New York City named Henry Bergh. Henry first got the idea of devoting his life to protecting animals when he was serving as a diplomat in Russia. While riding in a fancy horse-drawn coach, Henry saw a peasant beating a lame cart horse on the side of the road. The horse was injured and couldn't put weight on one of his legs, but the peasant was beating him to force him to continue pulling the cart. Henry ordered the man to stop. Russian peasants did not dare argue with noblemen, so the man did as he was told. In that moment Henry Bergh felt great joy at being able to help a suffering animal.

Henry resigned his diplomatic post and returned to the United States where he worked tirelessly to set up a society to protect animals and to convince the New York State Legislature to pass a law making it a crime to beat and overwork animals. The legislature not only passed a law but gave the ASPCA the police power to enforce the new law throughout the state. The ASPCA was the first animal protection organization in the Western Hemisphere, and Henry Bergh was the first person to enforce the law on the streets.

More than 140 years later, the ASPCA is still enforcing the anticruelty law through its Humane Law Enforcement officers—sometimes called "animal cops"—who investigate complaints and arrest people who are hurting or neglecting their animals. But the ASPCA protects animals in many other ways, too. One of the most important is through its Humane Education department. Humane education means teaching children to care about animals in their own homes and in their communities. It fosters kindness, compassion, and respect for animals, the environment, and other people. Humane education tries to build a sense of responsibility in young people to make the world a better, kinder place.

Here are some exciting ASPCA Humane Education programs to check out.

The **ASPCA Henry Bergh Children's Book Award** (www.aspca.org/bookaward) was set up to honor new books for children and young adults that promote compassion and respect for all living things. Each year the ASPCA gives awards in six categories: Companion Animals, Humane Heroes, Ecology and the Environment, Poetry, Young Adult, and Illustration. It gives separate awards for fiction and nonfiction. Winning books bear the Book Award seal, which consists of a silhouette of a horse and a gentleman wearing a top hat. The awards are named for Henry Bergh because he not only founded the ASPCA to prevent cruelty to animals, but also helped found the New York Society for the Prevention of Cruelty to Children in 1874. It was the first society to protect children from being beaten and starved by their parents. Henry Bergh understood that laws and police powers were not enough to ensure a humane society. Children must be treated kindly and taught to be kind to all living things in turn.

Henry's Book Club (www.aspca.org/henrysbookclub) was formed in 2008 as a way for kids who like animals *and* books to get together to read the ASPCA Henry Bergh Children's Book Award winners and discuss them as a group. Kids meet once a month in clubs that have been organized in schools or communities. The ASPCA provides polls, quizzes, and discussion questions for use at club meetings. Teens over 13 have the option of joining a virtual club through the ASPCA Online Community, where they can chat live about the books with teens across the country—and even with the authors, who join in from time to time as special guests!

ASPCA Kids, Animals, and Literature Bibliography (www.aspca.org/bibliography) is an online list of books about animals that the ASPCA Humane Education staff has reviewed and recommend as accurate, humane, and fun to read. It contains hundreds of titles and is easy to search by subject, title, author, or age, or by whether the book is fiction, nonfiction, or poetry. Winners of the ASPCA Henry Bergh Children's Book Awards are listed, too.

ASPCA Animaland (www.animaland.org) is the ASPCA's interactive web site for kids who love animals. There's a lot to learn at Animaland! Regular features include kids and animals in the news, information about careers working with animals, fun activities, Animal ABCs, and Ask Azula, where ASPCA experts answer kids' questions about animals.

Do Something (www.dosomething.org/aspca) is an online site that gives teens and tweens who want to make a difference lots of information and ideas about how to get involved in issues that matter to them. The ASPCA is the animal welfare partner of Do Something and gives $5,000 worth of grants each year to help fund worthy projects.

Index

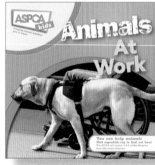

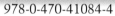